JUN - - 2012

HOW TO PREPARE FOR THE MEDICAL BOARDS

SECRETS FOR SUCCESS **ON USMLE STEP 1 AND COMLEX LEVEL 1**

HOW TO PREPARE FOR THE MEDICAL BOARDS

SECRETS FOR SUCCESS ON USMLE STEP 1 AND COMLEX LEVEL 1

ADELEKE T. ADESINA AND FAROOK W. TAHA

iUniverse, Inc.
Bloomington

How to Prepare for the Medical Boards
Secrets for Success on USMLE Step 1 and COMLEX Level 1

iUniverse books may be ordered through booksellers or by contacting:

iUniverse
1663 Liberty Drive
Bloomington, IN 47403
www.iuniverse.com
1-800-Authors (1-800-288-4677)

ISBN: 978-1-4502-9813-1 (sc)
ISBN: 978-1-4502-9814-8 (dj)
ISBN: 978-1-4502-9815-5 (e)

Library of Congress Control Number: 2011903335

Printed in the United States of America

iUniverse rev. date: 8/17/2011

Adeleke T. Adesina

University of Medicine and Dentistry, School of Osteopathic Medicine, New Jersey.
Class of 2012

Farook Wael Taha

University of Medicine and Dentistry, School of Osteopathic Medicine, New Jersey.
Class of 2012

Disclaimer

In preparing for this book, we used extreme caution to completely avoid violation of the terms and condition of the National Boards of Osteopathic Examiners (NBOME) and National Boards of Medical Examiners (NBME).

We contacted the NBOME office to review our book to make sure we did not violate their terms and conditions. We abided by the terms and conditions (V) in the NBOME Bulletin of Information, Candidate Confidentiality Agreement, published July 1, 2010.

We attempted to collaborate with the NBME office and requested they review the book in order to ensure no illegal content was revealed to the public, but they simply notified us about their terms and conditions, which we made every effort to adhere to.

Dedication

This book is dedicated to Almighty God, the author and finisher of our faith.

We would like to thank our loving families for their unending encouragement and support.

To me the ideal doctor would be a man endowed with profound knowledge of life and of the soul, intuitively divining any suffering or disorder of whatever kind, and restoring peace by his mere presence.

~Henri Amiel

Contents

Acknowledgments

We would like to thank the following people for their advice and contributions to the completion of this project.

Paul Krueger, DO
Associate Dean of Student Affairs and professor of Obstetrics and Gynecology,
University of Medicine and Dentistry New Jersey, School of Osteopathic Medicine

Jacqueline Giacobbe, MS. Ed
University of Medicine and Dentistry New Jersey, School of Osteopathic Medicine, Center for Teaching and Learning Academic Center

James White, PhD
UMDNJ School of Osteopathic Medicine, Neuroscience professor, author of *USMLE Road Map Neuroscience and Gross Anatomy*

John Barone, MD
Kaplan Pathology Instructor

Olufunmilayo Johnson, Pharm. D

Steven Agabeji, MD, Orthopedic Surgeon, Cincinnati Children's Hospital Medical Center, Assistant Professor at University of Cincinnati, Cincinnati, OH.
Author, *Step-Up to Medicine*

Preface

Dear Reader,

This book was written as a guide for medical students who are preparing for the USMLE Step 1 and COMLEX Level 1 Board exams. Our goal was to give you a step-wise approach to preparing for these two exams. USMLE Step 1 and COMLEX Level 1 (for osteopathic students) are two different examinations, and preparing for these exams is different.

If you are an allopathic or international medical graduate, you only need to focus on the USMLE section. Osteopathic students need to also understand how to study for the COMLEX Level 1, so a chapter is dedicated to that exam.

We first describe what the USMLE and COMLEX examinations are and what score ranges students can achieve on these two tests. The book includes a chapter on *First Aid for the USMLE Step 1,* which should be one of the primary sources for your Board preparation. We then discuss the importance of using questions; we highly recommend two of the best question banks on the market: USMLEWorld and Kaplan Question Bank.

Chapter 5, the integration chapter, is the key to using this book. This chapter demonstrates how students should prepare for the USMLE Step 1 and COMLEX Level 1 exams. You should read this chapter to fully understand this process; refer back to it as you proceed with your Board preparation.

We provided a sample Board schedule to serve as guide during your preparation; use it if it works for you. We offer a system-based learning method to cover the major topics tested on the Boards, according to *First Aid for the USMLE Step 1.* The book also offers a chapter for osteopathic students who are considering whether or not to take the USMLE Step 1 exam.

The book ends with a chapter focused primarily on how to survive medical school's rigorous education and on planning the most efficient way to maximize your medical education while still enjoying life during medical school.

We have been through the same situation you are in right now, and we are aware of your confusion and anxiety. We have written this book to improve your preparation.We hope this book sheds some light on how to survive the last few months of your Board preparation and helps you achieve the Board score you so wish for.

Confucius once said, *"The journey of a thousand miles begins with a step,"* and your journey is just about to begin.

Introduction

We wrote this book during our third year of medical school, after taking the USMLE Step 1 and COMLEX Level 1 exams. We experienced the dread every medical student feels before and after taking these licensing exams. Most of us often feel lost or confused. We realized that most students do not know how to utilize the resources and information available to do very well on these standardized exams. Most students have no systematic approach to preparing for these exams and end up developing anxiety issues over Boards.

We encounter many second-year medical students who ask for advice about how they should study for their Boards. Let us start by encouraging you—you will pass this exam. Many students before you have taken the test and succeeded; it is your turn to seize the moment! It is very *hard to fail*, whether you believe it or not. Even if you have taken the Boards once and did not pass, it was simply because you were either not ready or you made certain mistakes others have made prior to taking the test. But do not be discouraged—because you failed once does not define you. "What defines you is not what you do when you fail, what defines you is who you are when you rise after failing." (Author unknown)

This is a typical conversation: a second-year medical student asks for advice about Board preparation from an upper classman, who just finished taking the exam.

Are you familiar with this conversation? We bet you are! You are just like us at beginning of our second year of med school. We spoke to many third- and fourth-year medical students, asking them for the best way to study for Boards. They all seemed to have it figured out. Eight out of ten times we got this answer: "Memorize *First Aid* and do lots of questions." Maybe you feel like other students are not telling you something.

You have no idea how a student performed on his or her Boards, and no one will tell you either. So you do not know if he or she did the bare minimum to just pass the test or performed excellently on the exam. You dare not ask students what their Board scores are! We hope not. It is a personal thing. Most students only share their scores with a very few people. Do not take this personally either—after you have completed your Boards, you will understand better.

There must be more to the story, right? Yes, you are correct. There is, but no one spends the time to explain it to you; they want you to figure it all out by yourself. This approach gives most students the short stick. In order to clarify and thoroughly explain the nitty-gritty details that are often unexplained, we have created this book for your benefit ...So relax!

Instead of panicking, look for the resources, be self-disciplined, settle your mind, plan ahead, and get fired up for the biggest moment of your life. If you are one of those people who wants to excel on this exam, this book was written specially for you.

Read on!

Student Testimonials

Disclaimer

The students who wrote these testimonials willingly volunteered to share their scores and identity in this book. These are a few of the many students whom we have mentored and advised. We shared all the advice in this book with them before writing this book. We are now sharing this priceless masterpiece and the same experience with you the reader and we hope that your story will be similar these students too.

"I recently earned a 99 percentile on USMLE! I owe all of my success to the study strategy I received from Adeleke. I am fortunate to have such a knowledgeable friend who shared his efficient and effective plan with me. I am glad Adeleke is sharing those same secrets with many more people."

Ruth Arumala, MPH
Third-year Medical Student
UMDNJ-School of Osteopathic Medicine
Class of 2013

"I met Farook, one of the authors of this book, when I was a first year at UMDNJ-SOM. He gave me some pointers for my first year of medical school and found his advice to be priceless. So then second year comes along and the pressure of taking national board exams mounted. I went to Farook for some wisdom and he gave me a set of steps to followed, Farook reassured me that if I followed these steps that I would do very well in class and on my board exams. *I bought into the system and it worked wonders.* My grades went up from first year and I was really understanding and applying the concepts that were presented to us. Over time I found myself able to retain these concepts over all of second year. After second year, I sat for my USMLE and COMLEX-USA and scored 238/99 on the USMLE and 636 on the COMLEX-USA. Thanks Farook."

Yousef Hamdeh
UMDNJ-School of Osteopathic Medicine
Third Year Medical Student
Class of 2013

Chapter 1

USMLE and COMLEX

Before we begin discussing the USMLE Step 1 and COMLEX Level 1 examinations, let us focus on the main themes we want you to understand before reading this book. At no point during medical school should you ignore your coursework and core requirements for the sake of studying for the Boards!

1. Know that studying for your coursework *is* studying for the Boards. The associate dean for academic affairs and professor of obstetrics and gynecology at UMDNJ School of Osteopathic Medicine, Dr. Paul M. Krueger, DO, always says, "Data clearly showed that **how you perform in your schoolwork is the number one indicator of how you perform on your Board exams.**"

2. **You cannot graduate if you fail your coursework, so it is vital that you spend most of your time ensuring that you pass every class and all exams.**

The USMLE and COMLEX Exams

USMLE stands for the *United States Medical Licensing Exam*, which every allopathic medical student in the United States must take in order to be licensed to practice medicine. International students who wish to practice medicine must take this exam too. The passing score for USMLE is 189/75. While no one actually knows what the highest score for USMLE is, students have scored above 260/99 on the actual exam. Check the link for more details: http://www.usmle.org/Scores_Transcripts/minimum_passing.html

1

Adeleke T. Adesina and Farook W. Taha

COMLEX is the *Comprehensive Osteopathic Medical Licensing Exam*, required for DOs. Please be aware that **COMLEX is *not* equivalent to the USMLE. These exams are different.** DO students are allowed to sit for the USMLE exam if they wish to. The passing score for COMLEX-USA is 400/75. The highest score you can attain is 999/99. Check the link for more details: http://www.nbome.org/score-interpretation.asp

There are three parts to COMLEX and USMLE: Levels 1, 2, and 3 for the COMLEX and Steps 1, 2 and 3 for the USMLE. Every osteopathic medical student must pass all three levels of the COMLEX exam, and every allopathic medical student must pass all three levels of the USMLE exam.

So which of these exams is the most important and why? Many medical students will tell you how extremely important your Step 1 scores are. They are right, in a sense. There is a reason why every medical student focuses so much emphasis on USMLE Step 1 and COMLEX Level 1. **Not only is it important for your residency application! These are licensing exams required for you to 1) graduate from medical school, 2) be able to practice medicine in the United States.**

In the United States, medical school is a four-year program that includes first two years of basic and clinical sciences and two years of clinical rotations. The basic sciences taught in the first year include clinical biochemistry, anatomy and physiology, histology, embryology, preventive medicine, biostatistics, epidemiology, microbiology, osteopathic manipulative medicine (OMM, which only applies to DOs), et cetera.

The second year of medical school focuses on clinical medicine, pathology, pharmacology, immunology, geriatrics, pediatrics, psychiatry, and OMM (for DO students). After completing the second year, *you must take your boards. This is very important.* This is Step 1.

The third and fourth years of medical school involves students rotating in the hospital. This is the time when students get the opportunity to meet and interact with patients; they learn to take histories and perform proper physical exams. After the third year or at the beginning of fourth year, *you must take* COMLEX Level 2 and/or USMLE Step 2.

Then it is time to apply for residency. Remember when you had to prepare for your MCAT, get good scores, and apply to medical schools?

2

At this point, you are back at the same portal, which leads to a different route. Applications for residency can be very stressful for students, for various reasons. This is the time of your life where you have to make major decisions on what career path you want to embark on in medicine. You have completed all the clinical rotations, but sometimes you are still unsure which area of medicine in which you want to practice. This is normal: many students face this dilemma. You will eventually figure out what your passion is!

However, it's important to obtain a good residency position. What are the requirements to get in? Residency directors focus on several factors when you apply to their residency programs. Most medical students assume our Step 1 scores are the most important factor that will get us a residency. This idea is not the complete truth. Your Step 1 score is only one part of the application process. **Other requirements, such as clinical rotation grades, your personal statement, letters of recommendation, Step 2 scores, research and publications, and the interview process all factor into the equation.** Therefore, do not rely solely on your Step 1 scores as the key to get you into residency.

Getting to know the right people is another important piece of the puzzle. If you rotate at a hospital as a fourth-year medical student and work very hard, becoming a solid team member, you can make a strong impression on the attending physician, which might encourage the staff to consider you for a spot in their program. Therefore, the impression you make on your attending physician may allow you to be recognized as a great asset to their program. So is it all your scores? No! Is all about who you know? No! It is a combination of everything. Your entire application counts. **Do not ever give up your dreams for whatever specialty you are interested in because of your scores!**

However, Step 1 scores do have a strong influence when you apply to highly competitive residencies. Thousands of medical students are competing for the small pool of available spots. The exam scores start to matter. Although a solid Step 1 score is not the only thing you need to get into a good residency, it will get you to the door. For example, student A scores 245/99 on his USMLE or 700/96 on COMLEX, while student B scores 205/82 (USMLE) or 500/82 (COMLEX). If they both want to do plastic surgery, who do you think might get an interview first? The one with the higher score is most likely to get an interview, especially for highly competitive programs that lay more emphasis on Step 1 scores. Irrespective of what specialty you are interested in, you should aim for the highest score to make you a strong applicant for any residency of your choice.

Please refer to this website for two digit score conversion for COMLEX- http://www.nbome.org/CBTScoreConv/Default.aspx

Please note this UPDATE-

"Changes to USMLE Procedures for Reporting Scores

Starting July 1, 2011, USMLE transcripts reported through the ERAS reporting system will no longer include score results on the two-digit score scale. USMLE results will continue to be reported on the three-digit scale. This affects the Step 1, 2CK, and 3 examinations only; Step 2 CS will continue to be reported as pass or fail. **These changes do not alter the score required to pass or the difficulty of any of the USMLE Step examinations." (source- http://www.usmle.org/General-Information/ announcements.aspx?contentId=63)**

"The old brick road to the Oz known as residency is riddled with many twists and turns. The process is a test of endurance and strength of will and chances are, you will be a different person at the end of it than you were before you began your journey." ("USMLE Step 1 Reality YouTube Video," by Dr. Brian Bolante, theusmlezone.com)

U.S. MLE STEP I - Book of facts covering information of 1st 2 yrs, it should be repeatedly repeated studied. It states facts about USMLE, USMLE prepare for exam

US MLE step Step I

Chapter 2

What is *First Aid for the USMLE Step 1?*

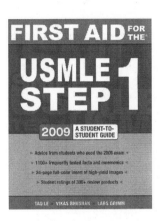

First Aid for the USMLE Step 1 is a familiar book to every medical student, both internationally and across the entire United States. It is the book of choice for studying for the Boards. **We strongly recommend that you (and everyone else) buy this book as early as possible in your medical school experience, if you want to do well on the COMLEX and/or USMLE.** Do not wait until a month before your Boards to buy this book. And do not buy the book and let it sit around without putting it to good use. Deadly idea …

First Aid for the USMLE Step 1 is not a textbook, as most students often think. We call it a book of facts, covering information from the first two years of medical school. If you open the book itself, it is not readable unless you have previously studied the material. It simply states facts about everything most likely to be tested on the COMLEX or USMLE. It offers effective mnemonics, which can help you retain information using a concise and easy method as you prepare for the exam. Some students find mnemonics helpful, while others do not. If you are a student who loves mnemonics, it will come in handy. *First Aid for the USMLE Step 1* offers high-yield pathology slides at the end of the book for review.

First Aid for the USMLE Step 1 is a comprehensive, high-yield review book that can help you to do well on the exam; we have written this book to help you get the most out of *First Aid for the USMLE Step 1*, offering you a different perspective on how to approach reading that allows you to make mental notes and associations that are not emphasized in the book.

Can students memorize all the facts in this book for the Boards? *No.* After studying for the Boards the effective way we will describe, you will be able to understand most of the materials that you need to excel on your Boards. We want you to realize that you cannot answer all Board questions correctly. So even if you memorize *First Aid*, you still won't be able to get all the answers correct. Read more to discover why.

Chapter 3

USMLEWorld and Kaplan Question Banks

Begin preparing for the Boards in advance, in small steps. We highly recommend that you purchase a year's subscription to The USMLEWorld Step 1 Qbank. Buy the subscription online: http://www.usmleworld.com.

Make sure you purchase it at the right time. Suppose you have to take the exam in June 21, 2012. *Do not* purchase the yearly Qbank subscription until July 15, 2011, which gives you a thirty-day buffer, in case you change your exam day. In that case, you'd still have access to the Qbank for practice. We understand some people might be opposed to this idea because it is quite expensive. However, we firmly believe it is a worth while investment. To reduce the cost, **buy a year's subscription only if you are absolutely sure you will be disciplined enough to use it throughout the year.** Some people buy the six-month subscription plan, while others subscribe for thirty days. We are fully aware of the financial burden many students already carry. If you cannot afford to buy the one-year subscription, make an effort to buy the six-month plan and begin studying early. Do whatever works for you, but we advise you to buy it as soon as possible. You will discover our reason as you continue this book.

The second year of medical school is highly intense. It is probably the most challenging, if not the hardest, part of your medical education. The year is so critical because you will learn various aspects of clinical medicine, pathology, and pharmacology in one year. It took the professors teaching these courses an entire career to master the material; and you are expected to memorize, understand, retain, and regurgitate the information in one year. That is madness, isn't it? Yes, we know—that's just medical school. Doctors are expected to *know everything*.

We know it is very difficult for most students to adjust to the intensity of medical school. Most students enter medical school with a different perspective toward studying. They suddenly find themselves in the midst of a nonstop flow of information, and they do not know how to deal with it. **If you are such a student, read chapter 13 on how to survive medical school before continuing.**

If you are already a very studious and well-prepared student, a student who has efficiently mastered the best and most efficient way to study any material given to you in a short time—and you still find time to sleep, eat, and exercise—then you are on the right track.

Please realize that studying for your second-year classes is equivalent to studying for Boards, since these are the materials you are most likely to be tested on for the exam. Students' coursework performance is the best predictor for their Board scores.

Although the second year of medical school does not provide enough time to balance studying for the Boards with your coursework, it is your responsibility to make the time. We disciplined ourselves to set aside one hour every night to do the USMLEWorld Step 1 Qbank questions. We started this as soon as we started the clinical medicine, pathology, and pharmacology courses. Since these courses are often taught in modules, it correlates well with the Qbank style.

Question: How do I start doing questions when I do not know what I am looking at yet?

Answer: That is why Boards study is different! As we told you at the beginning, forget everything you know about Board prep.

If you are on the cardiology module at your school, the ideal approach is to start doing ten cardio questions from the question bank every day. Do not underestimate ten questions. It will take you approximately ten to fifteen minutes to complete these ten questions from the question bank. It takes about thirty to forty-five minutes to review the answers for these ten questions. However, taking the test is not what is important. The most important thing is to **review every single question and answer from the question bank** you are using. Both the right and wrong answers must be reviewed in great detail. This is the best way to learn the material. In order words, preparing this way is the most efficient method of preparing for your actual board exam. ✓

The clinical vignette questions are much harder than you predict. The USMLEWorld Step 1 Qbank is probably one of the most difficult and most valuable question bank you can use to study for Boards. Although the questions are difficult, they help reinforce the very high-yield concepts for the exam. The Qbank also prepares you for how Board-style questions are often phrased.

Reviewing both your right and wrong answers to the Qbank questions is both very time consuming and painful. It is not an easy process. But *that is the only way you will know exactly what you need to know for the exam.* Most students have a habit of taking exams without reviewing the answers. This is *not* the way to study for Boards. USMLEWorld Step 1 Qbank is an excellent tool because it thoroughly explains the reasons why one answer is right and not the others. It also explains why the other answers are incorrect. These explanations are often long but very concise. At the end there is an educational objective summary, a short summary of what the test question wants you to know.

Question: How do I know if I am doing well when answering questions?

Answer: Initially, you will perform poorly on when you take USMLEWorld Step 1 Qbank tests. As a medical student, **you are *not* used to getting between 30 and 50 percent on an exam.** But with USMLEWorld Qbank, expect to be within that range, especially at the beginning. You do not know most of the material yet; even if you do, you are not familiar with how the concepts are tested in a Board-style clinical vignette format.

So do not feel depressed when your scores are really low. Most students who actually do well on the real exam score an average of 65 percent on USMLEWorld Step 1 Qbank.

If you are scoring between 40 and 50 percent from the start, you are actually doing really well and getting ready for the test. However, *do not* focus on your scores initially. Learn the material, understand the questions, and get used to the style of the exam.

Toward the end of your Board studies, you should begin to time yourself and mimic real exams conditions as you practice the Qbank. This will allow you to monitor your progress as exam time approaches.

Kaplan USMLE test preparation is another great resource for studying for the USMLE or COMLEX. It is almost identical to USMLEWorld in terms of style and format. If you enroll in the Kaplan Board review course, the question bank willbe included in your Kaplan course package. Kaplan is discussed later in the book.

Scoring an average 65 percent on the USMLEWorld Step 1 Qbank correlates to an estimated score of 237/ 99 ± 18 on USMLE. Check out this link:

http://www.clinicalreview.com/solutions/resources/usmle-score-calculator.html

Our simple rule for studying for the Boards is: "Get it wrong now, learn it cold, understand the mechanism, and get a good score when it counts."

Chapter 4

How to use *First Aid for the USMLE Step 1* effectively

You are doing questions fromUSMLEWorld or Kaplan Question bank; you reviewed the answers. Is that enough? *Absolutely not!* That is just the beginning.

1. **Buy the book.**

    Go online and buy the book. There are various websites to choose from, such as amazon.com, half.com, and borders.com. Always buy the most recent edition, which will correct errors from the previous editions. Check out the errors page online, to be sure you have the latest corrections, especially if you are using an older edition

2. **Go to a print shop, cut off the book binding, and add a three-hole punch through the book.**

    Insert the pages in a 2.5-inch binder. This will allow you to insert notes and extra materials inside your *First Aid*.

For more details, check out: www.prepareforthemedicalboards.com

3. **Add tabs.**

    Tabs are small plastic holders you can use to demarcate each chapter and section. This helps you easily flip through the book, saving time while looking up indexes and chapters. You can purchase tabs at your local stationery store.

4. **Use your *First Aid*.**

   Most students will buy *First Aid for the USMLE Step 1* and immediately start reading the book. It is *not a book*. Most students have a misconception about review books. *First Aid for the USMLE Step 1* is a collection of random high-yield facts that are commonly tested on the COMLEX and USMLE.

Warning: *Do not read* First Aid for the USMLE Step 1 *as a book*

The way you use *First Aid* is by first doing questions in the USMLEWorld or Kaplan question banks. Review the questions and answers. Then write those facts and explanations from USMLEWorld or Kaplan on the pages in your *First Aid for the USMLE Step 1* book where that information is given. This is an active learning process. Get involved!

Even if you decide to read *First Aid for the USMLE Step 1* first and then do the questions, you will still be scoring within 30% to 40% range on the practice exams. The book does not tell you much, if you do not know how to use it. Until you see how the material is tested in a question format, you have no idea what the facts in the book mean. Here's an example.

| Streptococcus Pneumoniae | Most common cause of: Meningitis Otits Media (in children) Pneumonia Sinusitis Encapsulated. IgA protease. | S. Pneumoniae MOPS are Most OPtochin sensitive. Pneumococcu s is associated with "rusty sputum, sepsis in sickle ⟷ cell anemia and splenectomy. |

Excerpt- 'Streptococcus Pneumoniae' page 147, from *First Aid for the USMLE Step 1* 2009 © 2009 Tao Le, Vikas Bhushan, Lars Grimm. Published by McGraw-Hill. This material is reproduced with permission of The McGraw-Hill Companies.

The following is a made-up sample question, not taken from a Board exam or any question bank. That is also true for all other questions in this book.

Question:

A nine-year African American boy presented with cough, a rusty sputum, and fever of 101.4 F. On physical exam he appears pale and lethargic. Vital signs reveal a blood pressure of 90/60 mmHg and warm extremities. Laboratory studies reveal hemoglobin of 8 mg/dl, hematocrit of 25 percent. He has a history of painful crisis, which is relieved with NSAIDs. What organism is this patient most likely susceptible to?

    A. Staph aureus

    B. Toxoplasmosis

    C. E. Coli

    D. Streptococcus pneumonia

    E. Ricketssiaricketssi

Answer: Streptococcus pneumonia

Explanation

The patient is African American who is anemic, with a history of painful crisis. You are expected to know that he has sickle cell anemia and hypotension from sepsis (his blood pressure is low). Since he is 9 years old, you should expect he does not have a functioning spleen, because such patients experience autosplenectomy from extensive hemolysis and splenomegaly since childhood. A patient without a spleen has an increased risk of developing infections from encapsulated organisms such as Strep pneumonia, Neisseria, H. influenza, and Klebsiella pneumonia. Therefore, the answer is **S. pneumonia.**

Educational Objective

Sickle anemic patients are susceptible to encapsulated organism such as Streptococcus pneumoniae, Neiserria, H. influenza and Klebsiella pneumonia.

Now you make notations of the objective in your copy of *First Aid.*

Do you see why "just reading the book" is almost useless? Most of us will read the fact: *Pneumococcus is associated with rusty sputum, sepsis in sickle cell anemia and splenectomy,* but have no idea how it will be tested.

This is why doing questions makes you see how the Boards wants you to understand the material. If you do many practice questions and sample NBME/NBOME questions, You will have an idea how boards questions are written and presented.

5. **Pick a color.**

    When you highlight a sentence or phrase in color, it means it is important. Pick your favorite color, perhaps green. *Use this color every time you do questions on your Qbank.* Highlight the facts tested in the USMLEWorld Step 1 Qbank in your *First Aid.* This approach reinforces the materials every time you open the book. So if something is in green, it is important: *there was a question on it—this is high-yield information.*

6. **The math.**

    If you do ten questions every day during your second year (except during exam time), in thirty days, you will have completed three hundred questions. If the semester were four months long, you would have completed approximately twelve hundred questions. Assuming you did not meet your goal at the end of the semester, you still have an opportunity to do so during the winter break, as well as wrap up any remaining questions in modules that you started but did not finish. By springtime, around April, you would probably have completed around two thousand questions. That means you would have completed the Qbank once even before hardcore Board studying begins.

Do you know how that feels? It feels good—you will be ahead of the game. You will have noticed most of the tricks and be familiar with different ways questions can be asked. You will be able to deduce what the exam question intends to test you on, and to a large extent your anxiety level will be reduced. This is simply because you took a whole year to prepare yourself for the COMLEX and USMLE, unlike many other students who just start to jump on the studying bandwagon in March or April. By the time you are almost done with the Qbank, your copy of *First Aid for the USMLE Step 1* should contain myriad details and be looking like a textbook that you can easily read and refer to for explanations. You will notice is that, by this time of the year, you are already accustomed to your *First Aid for the USMLE Step 1*; it is your personal inclusive review book for the Boards. It becomes your major asset as you prepare for the Boards.

We repeat: Do the USMLEWorld/Kaplan Step 1 Qbanks, write in your *First Aid*, and then read it, over and over and over.

Caveat: During the time of studying for your Boards, you should be aware that *First Aid for the USMLE Step 1* is not enough!

Although we are recommending that you do boards practice questions during your short winter break, or on weekends, please remember to always maintain a balance between your studies and other life chores and fun hobbies. It is extremely important to avoid getting burnt out early in this process.

First Aid for the USMLE Step 1 cannot be used alone to study; it is not the only book you need to do well on the test. Even USMLEWorld Step 1 Qbank and Kaplan Qbank are not enough. The book only contains about 75 percent of the material covered on the Boards. Some of the chapters in the book contain little information, and you will need supplementary materials to enhance your studying. Chapters such as pathology, microbiology, and behavioral science lack sufficient substance for you to fully understand those materials.

For instance, reading the microbiology section of *First Aid for the USMLE Step 1* is not enough for you to understand the whole picture. Supplementing it with *Microbiology Made Ridiculously Simple* will give you more information regarding the microorganism's structure, type of endo- or exotoxin released, antibiotic of choice, and pathogenesis of the diseases they cause.

Likewise, the pathology section is insufficient for the Boards. We cannot overemphasize the importance of reading *Rapid Review for Pathology* by Edward Goljan (see References). Dr. Goljan is an excellent Board review teacher, integrating the material in a concise format to help students understand how the materials will be tested on the exam. **We highly recommend this book for your Board studies.**

Towards the end of studying for Boards, about two days before your exam date, flip through *Rapid Review for Pathology* by Dr. Goljan; review all the side notes and look through all the pathology slides in the book. We found this very helpful for solidifying all the pathology information and recognizing the slides, should they appear on the Board exam.

Some students prefer *Board Review Series (BRS) Pathology*. Either the Goljan *Pathology* or *BRS Pathology* is a great resource for studying. Note: Goljan has more information in his book and more pathology slides than *BRS Pathology*. Use whichever one you are comfortable with. Another great source for studying pathology is attending Kaplan pathology live lectures by Dr. John Barone. We had a great experience with his lectures; he truly does an excellent job teaching you pathology material that is high yield for Boards. He provides students with awesome mnemonics and simplified approach to learning difficult concepts. We refer to him as the "epiphany of academia."

You might want to review some biochemistry pathways through the Kaplan biochemistry book. It is an excellent resource for biochemistry for the Boards. If you subscribe to Kaplan Board review course, the biochemistry videos offered are the best, in our opinion. The professor makes you fall in love with biochemistry. He emphasizes all the high-yield points for the National Boards; you will feel very prepared. If you do not have access to this, do not panic. Try to borrow the book from anyone who has it, or use another biochemistry resource. There are tons of resources online to help you out (Check the resources section of this book for details).

Do not underestimate the importance of the behavioral science, epidemiology, and ethics sections. Many students ignore or don't prepare sufficiently for these sections. Make sure you read books on behavioral science and biostatistics, if you feel that *First Aid* material is not sufficient. USMLEWorld also added a new biostatistics question bank to their software; you might want to purchase it. Kaplan also provides great questions to help you practice. You can improve your score by spending some time on these topics, and any other topics you are weak with. **Always focus on your weaks areas when studying.**

If you want to invest time to study embryology, we recommend that you practice all the USMLEWorld or Kaplan question banks, after reviewing the section in *First Aid*. The explanations for the answers are more than enough. However, if you want to study still more embryology, you can use other sources to supplement. Check out our High-Yield Resource page for more details on resources.

We were fortunate enough to have the right resources to prepare for Boards. We received a great amount of materials from our upper classmen, and cannot emphasize enough how important it is for you to do the same. You should make every effort to look for great resources that others have tried and strongly recommended. This will help you greatly during your board preparation process. Again, different resources work for different students. If a resource is not working for you, stop using it and try another one.

As emphasized in this book, the USMLEWorld or Kaplan Question Bank is the best way to go to prepare for the USMLE and COMLEX. Ideally, you should go through the Question Bank twice. The first time do ten module-specific questions a night, following your second-year schedule. The second time should be at the end of the school year, after you have completed the entire Qbank and *First Aid* at least once. If you have more time, the Kaplan USMLE question bank offers more "media questions" (pictures, heart sounds, and slides) that will help with Board preparation to a great extent.

Students who are very efficient with their time may have the USMLEWorld Qbank completed by the end of their second year (April in most schools). They use the rest of April and some of May to do at least a hundred questions a night to complete the entire Kaplan USMLE question bank, which should go faster because they gained a tremendous amount of information from going through USMLEWorld. Then in June, they go through USMLEWorld Qbank the second time in a timed setting, now choosing random questions covering all the topics.

Once you have already reviewed these questions and have written the explanations down, going through USMLEWorld the second time should be quick and easy, and you will definitely score higher because of your efforts. In June, plan to do around two hundred questions a night. That is why it is important to be efficient and to write everything down the first time you go through USMLEWorld Question Bank. The questions you get wrong the second time will point to your areas of weakness and alert you to focus on those areas.

Doing one hundred USMLEWorld questions a night in June means you can complete the Question Bank for the second time by the middle of June. At that point, you should be ready to wrap up Board preparation and go "slay the beast."

If you are struggling to keep up with the school material, **do not risk your education!** Focus on passing every class and exam, because nothing is worse than failing your class—that is to be avoided! You will not be allowed to take the Boards if you fail. So learn the coursework material very well and understand it, and then you won't struggle to try to relearn the material during Board studying time. Doing well in your courses will save you time and effort, thus making the studying process much easier.

For osteopathic students, Kaplan COMLEX question bank and COMBANK are resources available to study for the COMLEX. You should make good use of these question banks to help you prepare for the COMLEX-USA Level 1 exam. Although the USMLEWorld and Kaplan USMLE question banks are great resources for their content, they are not the best way to adapt to the style of the questions in COMLEX. **DO students, please remember—USMLE Step 1 is not the same as COMLEX Level 1, and signing up for both is signing up for two different exams. You can easily see that if you look at NBME/NBOME sample questions.**

**Remember, you must do well in your second-year classes. That is why we insist that our technique works best for students who are already comfortable with time management skills and have learned how to survive medical school without falling behind and without being easily overwhelmed.

Chapter 5

The integration

Studying for the board exam has a distinctive methodology, which requires you to make abstract observations and assumptions and, most importantly, integrate concepts as to how each disease process relates to each other. We will discuss that shortly.

Medicine is a study of human pathophysiological phenomenon, integrated into one science. In medical school, you learn biochemistry, microbiology, immunology, anatomy and physiology, pathology, pharmacology, and clinical medicine. These classes are taught as separate entities and provide students with all the knowledge they need to be able to apply the information in a clinical setting.

However, as most of you know, getting through medical school itself is a hassle. Most students struggle through the rigorous first two years of medical school and emerge confused. Most of us do not have to time to think about what we are learning but just try to get through every exam. Dr. Goljan once compared medical students to the cell cycle, constantly in G1-S / G2-M phases due to weekly exams. After exams are over, they resort to their G0 phase, resting until the next exam approaches. This is why some medical students fail to understand that all the information they are been taught is part of a whole! But first you have to learn each aspect as an individual entity. Later, down the line, it is up to you to integrate it all together, because most medical schools do not do a great job of integrating the material for you.

Basically, when you learn the structure (anatomy) and function (physiology) of the human body, it allows you to understand the norms. However, when things go wrong (pathology), you can identify the dysfunction and what caused it (microbiology) and determine how to fix it, either with the use of medications (pharmacology), allowing the body to heal itself (immunology), or correcting with manipulation (OMM) or surgery, if necessary. That is medicine in a nutshell.

Unfortunately, integration of the information is not well taught. Somehow, you are expected to figure that out. You must learn how to see the big picture and think in that perspective. Patients do not present with symptoms and offer written multiple choice options on their forehead stating the diseases they might have. You are the doctor, and you are supposed to figure that out. If you understand the mechanisms, if you know the "*whys*" and not just the "*whats*", you will be far ahead of the curve. Memorization of facts is not the best way for you study as a medical student. **When you begin studying for boards, please make sure you focus on understanding mechanisms, mechanisms, mechanisms, and mechanisms! That is the key!**

So if it is all about the why, shouldn't you be able to simply read the *First Aid for the USMLE Step 1* and do well? As we said before: *no!* That is not true at all. We want you to see the *First Aid for the USMLE Step 1* book as a puzzle. The book contains many hints and facts. At the end, you should be able to put these puzzles together and see the connections throughout the book.

Dissecting *First Aid for the USMLE* and integrating the concepts

Let us take a look at the book, using the 2009 edition. You might have an updated edition, but the content does not differ extensively. The authors correct a few errors and add new content. The book offers advice for medical students at the beginning and includes other valuable information regarding the Board exam.

The subjects covered in *First Aid* are:

GENERAL PRINCIPLES	ORGAN SYSTEMS
Behavioral Science	Cardiovascular
Biochemistry	Endocrine
Embryology	Gastrointestinal
Microbiology	Hematology and Oncology
Immunology	Musculoskeletal and Connective Tissue
Pathology	Neurology
Pharmacology	Psychiatry

Here are some key issues with *First Aid*. First, many concepts are covered in the course of several chapters, due to their clinical association with various organ systems throughout the book. Here's an example.

In the biochemistry chapter, on pg. 92, autosomal trisomies are discussed in extensive detail. Down syndrome is perfect example. But pg. 92 does not include everything you need to know about Down syndrome for the Boards. It is also covered on pg. 93, 216, 259, 315, 402, 497, 499, and 503.

Down Syndrome (trisomy 21)1:700	Findings: mental retardation, flat facies, prominent epicanthal folds, simian crease (see Image 100), gap between 1ˢᵗ 2 toes, duodenal atresia, congenital heart disease (most commonly septum primum-type ASD). Associated with increased risk of ALL and Alzheimer's disease (>35 years of age).	Drinking age (21). Most common Chromosomal disorder and most common cause of congenital maternal retardation. Results of pregnancy quad screen: dec. alpha-fetoprotein, inc. beta-hCG, dec. estriol, inc. inhibin A. Ultrasound shows increased nuchal translucency.
	95% of cases due to meiotic nondisjunction of homologous chromosomes (associated with advanced maternal age, from 1:1500 in women <20 to 1:25 in women >45). 4% of cases due to robertsonian translocation. 1% of cases due to Down Mosaicism (no maternal association).	

Excerpt- 'Down Syndrome, pg. 92, from *First Aid for the USMLE Step 1* 2009, Tao Le, Vikas Bhushan, Lars Grimm, the McGraw-Hill Companies. This material is reproduced with permission of The McGraw-Hill Companies.

If the syndrome is covered on eight different pages in the book, it must be very important.

Second, connecting the dots is a key. Down syndrome is one disease with several pathological manifestations in different organ systems. How should you understand disease processes for Boards?

(We use Down syndrome as a classical example here but this can apply to any other disease process).

Down syndrome (trisomy 21) is the most common chromosomal disorder and most common cause of congenital mental retardation.

Mechanism/pathogenesis

Ninety-five percent of cases are due to meiotic non-disjunction of homologous chromosomes (associated with advanced maternal age; from 1:1500 in women age < 20 to 1:25 in women age > 45. Four percent can be due to robertsonian translocation.

Physical findings

Include flat faces, prominent epicanthal folds, single simian crease, and gaps between the first two toes.

Now that you understand the mechanism, the Boards may test you about every organ system's pathology associated with the disease. Let us break it down by organ systems.

a. **Neurology:** By age 35, a patient with Down syndrome has an increased risk of developing Alzheimer's disease. Refer to pg. 402 (neurology-anatomy and physiology section) **Alzheimer's:** Amyloid precursor protein on chromosome 21 (p-App gene) is associated with Alzheimer's disease. Keep in mind that you probably read page 95 a while ago and may forget that you are reading something similar on page 402.

b. **Cardiology:** The most common congenital heart defects found in the Down syndrome patient are ventricular septal defect (VSD), atrial septal defect (ASD), and atrioventricularseptal defect (endocardiaccushing defect). Now, refer to page 259, "Congenital cardiac defect associations."Down syndrome is mentioned again, to remind you of cardiac anomalies associated with Down syndrome.

c. **Gastrointestinal system:** page 315; Duodenal atresia and hirschrungs disease are highly associated with Down syndrome.

d. **Hematology and oncology:** page 95 and 216. Down syndrome patients have an increased risk of developing acute lymphoblastic leukemia (ALL).

The Big Picture

Sample USMLE-style Questions (we made up this question)

1. A neonate was delivered at thirty-eight weeks gestation with no pregnancy complications. The mother did not receive any prenatal care prior to delivery. On physical exam, the physician noted a flat prominent face, a simian crease and epicanthal fold, and a 3/6 loud

holosystolic murmur at the left lower sternal border. What is the most likely diagnosis?

   a. Trisomy 18

   b. Trisomy 13

   c. Trisomy 21

   d. Fragile X

   e. Digeorge syndrome

Answer: Trisomy 21.

This is the only disease associated with the physical examination findings of a flat face, prominent epicanthal folds, single simian crease, and gaps between the first two toes.

2. A neonate was delivered at thirty-eight weeks gestation to a forty-year-old mother with no pregnancy complications. The mother did not receive any prenatal care prior to delivery. On physical exam, the physician noted a flat prominent face, a simian crease and epicanthal fold, and a 3/6 loud holosystolic murmur at the left lower sternal border. Four days after birth the mother of the baby noted bilious vomiting with a distended abdomen. X-ray of the abdomen shows a "double bubble sign." What is cause of the neonate's abdominal distention?

   a. Meconium ileus

   b. Duodenal atresia

   c. Hirsprungs disease

   d. Constipation

   e. Pyloric stenosis

Answer: Duodenal atresia is associated with double bubble sign on an x-ray and is an increased risk in Down syndrome patients.

3. A neonate was delivered at thirty-eight weeks gestation with no pregnancy complications. The mother did not receive any prenatal care prior to delivery. On physical exam, the physician noted a flat prominent face, a simian crease and epicanthal fold, a wide

gap between first and second toe. This baby is at risk of what neurologic disease as he gets older?

a. Picks disease

b. Tuberous sclerosis

c. Alzheimer's disease

d. Neurofibromatosis type 2

e. Friedreich's ataxia

Answer: Alzheimer's. Down syndrome patients have an increased risk of developing early onset Alzheimer's later in life.

4. A thirty-eight-year-old Caucasian presents to her primary care physician's office at sixteen weeks pregnant. The physician performed ultrasound and noted increased nuchal translucency. What do you expect the result of the pregnancy quad screen to be?

	β-hCG	α fetoprotein	Estriol A	Inhibin
A	↑	↓	↓	↑
B	↓	↓	↓	↓
C	↓	↓	↑	↑
D	↑	↓	↑	↑

Answer: A

Down syndrome quad screen results are: high B-hCG, high Inhibin A, low alpha-fetoprotein and low estriol. Increased nuchal translucency is a classic finding in a Down syndrome fetus on ultrasound.

Example Two

Here is another example of integrated concepts. In *First Aid for the USMLE Step 1,* Hemochromatosis appears on pages 205,264,318, and 320. This outlines the association and connections between effects of the disease on various organ systems.

Hemochromatosis is an autosomal recessive disease in which iron is absorbed beyond the body's needs and there is no saturation point, leading to accumulation of iron in different parts of the body, starting with the liver. The excess iron deposition causes inflammation, fibrosis, and tissue damage. The following are systemic manifestation of the disease.

a. GI (pg. 318 and 320): Liver and pancreas are damaged. Hepatomegaly, liver cirrhosis, causes the typical signs and symptoms of portal HTN and liver failure, and increased risk of hepatocellular carcinoma. In the pancreas, the damage leads to destruction of the islet cells, resulting in diabetes mellitus (or at least glucose intolerance due to decreased insulin secretion).

b. Cardio (pg. 264): Heart failure due to restrictive cardiomyopathy. The patient will present with signs and symptoms of both left-sided and right-sided heart failure. Conduction defects are also possible.

C. Musculoskeletal (Pg. 320): Arthropathy due to iron being deposited in the joints.

d. Skin (pg. 320): "hyperpigmentation" of the skin.

E. Other: Testicular atrophy and impotence, hypopituitarism, and increase risk of infection by iron-loving bacteria such as *vibrio vulnificus and yersinia.* (Other manifestations are available from different review books)

Sample Board-style Questions

1. A twenty-four-year old male presents with polyuria and polydyspia. He mentions that his friends have noticed he is getting tanner. He is also lethargic. Which of the following is likely to help with the diagnosis?

a) Chest x-ray

b) Echocardiogram

c) Kidney biopsy

d) Liver biopsy

e) Glucose tolerance test

Answer: D. Liver biopsy

Explanation

The question is indirectly asking you what the most likely pathology associated with hemochromatosis is, which is diabetes. The patient has signs of polyuria, polydipsia, and tanning (iron deposition on the skin). Ordering a glucose tolerance test will show elevated blood sugar (hyperglycemia) >126mg/dl fasting blood sugar. However, his diabetes is secondary to destruction of the pancreas by iron deposition. The best way to diagnose hemochromatosis is a liver biopsy.

4. A thirty-three-year-old Caucasian American presented to his family physician complaining of impotence and loss of libido. He has a past medical history of diabetes, arthritis, congestive heart failure, and hyperpigmentation of his skin. Which of the following lab result will most likely confirm his diagnosis of hemochromatosis?

	Iron	Ferritin	Transferrin saturation	TIBC
A	↑	↓	↓	↑
B	↓	↓	↓	↓
C	↓	↓	↑	↑
D	↑	↑	↑	↓

Answer: D

The patient has hemochromatosis, so you would expect elevated iron levels, ferritin, and transferrin saturation, but low total iron binding capacity.

Example Three

In *First Aid for the USMLE Step 1* 2009, Turner syndrome (pages 259, 293, 461, 497, 503) is described as a sex chromosomal disorder in females who have XO chromosomes. The characteristic features are short stature, broad chest, ovarian dysgenesis, amenorrhea, preductal coarctation of the aorta, no barr body, horseshoe kidney, cystic hygromas, and lymphedema of the hands and feet.

Pathophysiology

Turner syndrome is caused by a mitotic error during early development (45 XO). These patients have low estrogen, which leads to increase in LH and FSH.

However, learning the above facts is not enough; Turner syndrome can present differently.

1. A twenty-one-year-old female presents to the office, complaining she never had her period. On physical exam, she is forty-four inches tall with a broad chest and widely spaced nipples. Her hands and feet appear edematous. What chromosomal finding are you most likely see in this patient?

    a. 44XXY

    b. 45XYY

    c. 46XX

    Turner → d. 45XO

    Syndrome e. 47XXX

Answer: D

This is a classic presentation of Turner syndrome. The patient presented with short stature, broad chest, and widely spaced nipples. Her hands and feet appear edematous. Most Turner syndrome patients have 45XO chromosomal abnormalities.

2. A twenty-one-year-old female presents to the office, complaining she never had her period. On physical exam, she is forty-four inches tall, with a broad chest and widely spaced nipples. Her hands and feet appear edematous. Intravenous pyelogram revealed horseshoe kidney. Which anatomic structure is preventing the kidneys from ascending in this patient?

    a. Superior mesenteric artery

    b. Celiac artery

    c. Inferior vena cava

    d. Inferior mesenteric artery

    e. External iliac vein

Answer: D

The image shows a bilateral horseshoe kidney, which is common in Turner syndrome patients. The two kidneys are obstructed by the inferior mesenteric artery, which prevents these structures from ascending during development.

3. A twenty-one-year-old female presents to the office complaining she never had her period. On physical exam, she is forty-four inches tall, with a broad chest and widely spaced nipples. Her hands and feet appear edematous. Her blood pressure in her left arm was 160/95 mm Hg and left leg was 90/60 mm Hg, with weak pulses in her legs. What cardiac abnormality do you suspect in this patient?

    a. Patent ductusarteriosus

    b. VSD

    c. Coarctation of the aorta.

    d. ASD

    e. Tetrology of fallot

Answer: C

Coarctation of the aorta is highly associated with Turner syndrome. Such patients also have bicuspid valves, which can result in aortic regurgitation. You can locate this integration in the cardio section of your *First Aid*, where coarctation of the aorta is discussed.

Can you see how important it is to not only know the pathogenesis of disease process, but every single association with each disease? There are so many ways a single concept can be tested. As you can see from the test question examples above, learning the pathogenesis is not enough; they expect you to know all the associations and possible clinical presentations.

The authors of *First Aid for the USMLE Step 1* do not emphasize the importance of integration when they present the material. They list the associations in different sections of the book; however, in our experience, when you read the book, you miss the trend. It is your responsibility to integrate the facts and connect the dots.

The best resources that actually integrate *First Aid for USMLE Step 1* are either the USMLEWorld or Kaplan question bank. The more questions you practice, the more you learn how to integrate the material so you are able to handle two- to three-step thought process questions. As a medical student, you are expected to have the knowledge and be able to apply it to the next step. Not only do you have to commit a lot of the facts to memory, but you have to take it a step further and apply the knowledge to clinical scenarios. Once you master this, you have mastered the art of preparing for the exam. Next, we will discuss the art of taking the test in a more efficient way. In the following chapter, we will discuss strategies and techniques that help you easily answer Board questions.

Chapter 6

Studying Practice Questions

How do I read questions and maximize my time with Board questions?

Let's face it. There has to be a good system for addressing practice questions. Questions are designed so they have a consistent pattern. A clinical vignette/scenariois followed by a question stem and then options. However, if you are not aware of these patterns, you will most likely run out of time or not finish each block.

There are distracters in questions and main ideas that you should be looking for in questions. Before we begin, we want to emphasize that the exam covers every subject that you have studied in the *First Aid USMLE Step 1* book. However, every new question stems from a different chapter—so how do you narrow your focus without panicking or wondering how to begin to answer a question?

The Strategy

Sample USMLE-style question

A four-year-old Caucasian male present to the clinic with fever of 102°F, cough, and a foul-smelling green mucopurulent discharge lasting for the past three days. His parents noticed his stool has been floating in the toilet, and he has not been growing well compared to his peers. The mother reports his skin tasted salty. On physical exam, he shows signs of weakened bones and malnourishment. Lung exam shows decreased breath sound, rales, increased tactile fremitus, and egophony in the right middle lobe; there is no wheezing. What organism most likely caused the patient's symptoms?

33

A. streptococcus pneumonia

B. Serraciamarcessens

C. Pseudomonas aeroginosa

D. Klebsiella pneumonia

E. Enterococcus

Answer: Choice C

1. Take a quick glance at the options first

This is extremely important. This allows you to narrow down what the question wants you to know. This is a microbiology question. Briefly looking over the answer choices ahead of time for a few seconds narrows your focus to microbiology, not something else.

2. Read the last sentence of the paragraph.

Many times you do not need to read the entire question to figure out the answer to the question. For instance:

A twelve-year-old African American female presents with chest pain, knee pain and weakness, and shortness of breath. The patient reports she gets "painful crisis" episodes and sometimes requires hospitalization. She reports having her spleen removed when she was ten because of her sickle cell disease. Lab shows Hb 7.5. What medication is most likely to increase the concentration of HbF in sickle cell patients?

A. Amiodorone

B. Acetaminophen

C. Busulfan

D. Hydroxyurea

E. Atenolol

As you can see, if you used the "glance at the answer first" approach, you can quickly assume this is a pharmacology question. Next, read the last sentence of the question stem: "What medication is most likely to increase the concentration of HbF in sickle cell patients?" Hydroxyurea is the medication of choice used for sickle cell patients to increase the

34

concentration of HbF in order to improve oxygen delivery to tissues and prevent vaso-occlusive crisis.

If you still cannot figure out the answer, go to the beginning of the question. If you are using USMLEWorld or Kaplan Question banks, you can highlight words and cross out answers. This is an important tool, one we think most students do not make good use of. Highlighting is a critical tool because it allows you to focus on the main signs and symptoms that the patient in the question presents with. For example:

A four–year-old Caucasian male presents to the clinic with a fever of 102°F, a cough, and foul-smelling green mucopurulent discharge lasting for the past three days. The parents noticed his stool tends to float in the toilet, and he has not been growing well compared to his peers. The mother reports his skin tastes salty. On physical exam, he shows signs of weakened bones and malnourishment. Lung exam shows decreased breath sounds, rales, increased tactile fremitus, and egophony in right middle lobe; no wheezing is appreciated. What organism is most likely caused the patients symptoms?

Can you see why highlighting is important? We have highlighted the main signs and symptoms in the question, which allows you to see what is important and ignore the distractors. We can basically summarize the key points of this question as:

"A four–year-old Caucasian male with fever, cough, foul green discharge, steatorrhea, salty skin, failure to thrive, with pneumonia."

What do you think this child has? Cystic fibrosis, of course!

Questions always give you hints and key points to narrow down the disease in question. So watch carefully for the description of disease processes, because they are literally giving it away. For instance,

a. A four–year-old Caucasian male—Pay close attention to ethnicity and age of the patient. If ethnicity is mentioned in a question, do not ignore it. It is a very important clue, due to the association between certain diseases and their prevalence in specific ethnic groups. For example, cystic fibrosis is more common in Caucasians, whereas sickle cell anemia is more prevalent among African Americans.

b. "Fever 102°F, cough, foul-smelling green mucopurulent discharge lasting for the past three days…decreased breath sound, rales, increased tactile fremitus, and egophony in right middle lobe" are signs of bacterial pneumonia

c. Steatorrhea indicates malabsorption and pancreatic enzyme deficiency, lipase for lipid digestion.

d. Weakened bones (osteomalacia) indicates fat-soluble vitamin deficiency of vitamin D

e. Salty skin lack of reabsorption of chloride from sweat.

These represent the clues that are usually given in the question stem. Watch carefully for these descriptions, because they point you in the right direction. How do you get good at this? **By practicing as many questions as you can.** Can you see how important doing questions is?

Chapter 7

Studying for the Boards

Here's a story that relates to studying for the Boards and illustrates the maxim, "To fail to prepare is to prepare to fail."

A town crier once came to a small village and warned the people of an impending war that might wipe out their entire population. The town crier said, however, it would be two years before the war began. The people were shocked but replied, "We will be ready in two years." Since it was still two years ahead, they did not have to worry until then. A paraplegic leper overheard the message and decided to start crawling slowly to safety. Two years passed by, and the people forgot. The war came and wiped out the entire population. Only the leper survived.

What is the point of the story? Many students behave like the people of this small village. We all know that we have to take the COMLEX/USMLE. Early preparation is one the most valuable things any medical student who really wants to perform well on these exams should do.

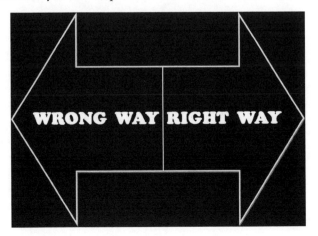

As a student, ever since you learned how to read and write you are accustomed to studying in a linear fashion. You have attended schools where you were given information that you were instructed to memorize and were told there would be an exam. You did exactly as you were told and you regurgitated the answers back, word for word. You got an A. And people said you were smart. You have done this for as long as you can recall. It always worked. It never failed. Right?

However, *for Boards, it will not work*. We are sorry—we know we just broke your heart. Memorization and regurgitation is the worst approach; it will lead to barely passing, or even failing the test. We call it the "wrong way"! Board exams are not your typical medical school exams, where you stay up all night memorizing every origin and insertion of a muscle or biochemical pathway under the sun. Look at NBME/NBOME sample questions and you will see it is more than memorization. If it was a memorization exam, everyone would score a 260/99 or 750/99, and we would all get into dermatology and neurosurgery, if we chose. But this is not the case.

Here is the secret; it is the opposite of how you used to learn. **In order to do well on Boards, you literally have to move inside the mind of the exam writers and think exactly like them.** You'll want to know how to do that, right? It is a skill that you will acquire after studying the tips we offer in this book.

The Rules

1. **Make a decision and set a *goal*.** 2 60 / 99

Most of us do not realize that in order to accomplish anything in life, **you must *have goals.*** As a medical student, ask yourself this question: How well do you want to do on this exam? Do you just want to pass with scores of 189/75 or 400/75, or do you want to excel and rock this exam with a 240/99 or 600/89? As a human, you have the potential to do anything. Often you think you have reached the limit of how far you can go, but there is room for much more. **We strongly urge you to set realistic and achievable goals.**

We fully understand everyone's goals are different. However, when we embarked on our preparation, we said to ourselves: want to score a 260/99 on the USMLE exam. That was the *goal!* It sounds like we are high achievers, but we noticed that people who established a high expectation and worked toward it might not necessarily reach that goal, but more often than not, they got close to such a goal. So, aim high, strive for the best, and you will be satisfied with your result.

If your goal is simply to pass the exam, you should aim for it and achieve it. For some, this is a milestone of achievement; for others it may be different. We are by no means telling you what you should do, but rather describing what we decided as a goal. Whatever it is, set your goals, be fervent, and persevere until you achieve it—that will make all the difference.

"Reach for the moon. Even if you miss it, you will land among the stars." -Les Brown-

2. **Write your goal down.**

Most of us have a goal in mind; we only talk about it. But people who write down their goals have a higher chance of achieving them. So, write down your goals in a diary, a paper, or a secret place.

3. **Be disciplined, and have a positive attitude toward your preparation**.

Doing well on Boards requires some mental tweaking. Most students are anxious about taking Boards. They panic and are very anxious about the test. The best favor you can do for yourself is to have a positive attitude. Remind yourself daily that you will do well on the exam. Do not associate with friends who are overly anxious and who will raise your blood pressure about taking the exam.

Discipline is one of the most essential tools any physician-to-be should acquire. Be very disciplined, plan your schedule wisely, and spend your time judiciously throughout your second year. Remember, you do not get a second chance at this, unless you fail.

4. **Know yourself, start early, and do not procrastinate.**

Know yourself. It is simple. If you know you are not a last-minute learner, if you are someone who needs a good amount of time to master any information, then do not fool yourself. Starting early is the right way for you. Even if you are a last-minute learner, someone who can cram in lots of information in a short time, save yourself some anxiety by starting early. You have nothing to lose.

One of the best piece of advice we received from some upperclassmen was that the ideal way to get your mind ready for this exam was to start early and start small.

Board Review Courses

There are many courses out there for Boards review. The most well-known ones are Kaplan, Falcon, PASS Program, and Doctors in Training. Some schools make these courses mandatory for all students; others do not. Do you really need one?

The main benefit of such courses is that they provide structure and discipline for those students who need a classroom instructor to help them study for the exam. These programs also provide good questions banks or Qbooks. Other benefits include the lectures that cover the high-yield topics in each discipline. Please understand these lectures will not cover everything you need to know for the test. There simply is not enough time to squeeze two years worth of medical school material into a few weeks. If their schedule says three days are assigned for pathology, do *not* put off studying pathology until then, assuming they are going to cover all the material you need to know. Basically the instructors will pick and choose what they feel is high-yield, based on the sample questions NBME or NBOME put out yearly. Another benefit is that these courses usually provide you books and video lectures to cover most of the material on your Boards. Is it smart to read all the books and watch all the videos? Probably not, given that most students have about a month to seven weeks of free time between the end of school and the recommended dates to take those exams. And it should be obvious by the end of the first year which subjects you are weak at.

For example, many people feel weak in biochemistry. Well, maybe this is a topic you need to cover entirely, either through the videos or the books. Personally, we believe the videos provided by these review courses are a great study resource, instead of reading a whole book, especially because the video will emphasize a few topics over others: for example, which enzymes you need to remember for which pathways in biochemistry. Obviously, if you are strong in a certain topic, do not waste time reviewing it from scratch; instead, jump to the questions and test how well you know it.

If, and only if, you find you are getting many questions wrong in a certain topic you thought you knew—for example, you got all the urea cycle questions wrong—then that is the time to watch the video or read the section on the urea cycle, not the entire biochemistry text. *Imp*

Most of these courses give you their books and grant you access to their online question bank sometime around December of your second year. The smartest thing to do is sit with your *First Aid for the USMLE Step 1*, or whatever review book you are using, identify your strengths and weaknesses, and make a list of the topics you need to review. You might find that you need to review everything from first year, and that is okay. The point of doing this self-assessment is to realize what you need to work on as early as possible. *Imp*

Make goals and plan early for how you are going to fit reviewing these topics within your busy second-year schedule. Maybe you will dedicate

Sundays to Boards reviews, or maybe you prefer an hour each night. The point is, make use of these resources early, and work on your weak points January through April. Keep in mind, as we've discussed, you should be doing questions every night regardless.

There is no excuse to pick between doing USMLEWorld questions on the topics you are covering in medical school versus reviewing first-year material. You should be able to do both if you plan carefully and study efficiently. We personally did our school studying and USMLEWorld questions about that material every night, and starting in January we dedicated Sundays to Board prep to study and review the material we felt we were weak at. By the middle of April we were almost finished reviewing all this material.

It's a great feeling to know that your review book of choice has everything you need, you have reviewed most of the material, and you still have at least two months. If you achieve that, then in May and June you are mainly doing questions, as well as attending the review lectures you feel you can use some extra tips on. As mentioned earlier, we used the last two months to complete the Kaplan question bank, and then went back to do USMLEWorld question bank for the second time around.

If the review course is mandatory, make good use of it, because it can be a great asset to your studying and Boards preparation. If it is not mandatory, then it is up to you; you know yourself best. If you can find a way to access this information (perhaps through friends or upper classmen), and you have a good question bank, maybe you will not need it. We will leave it up to you to evaluate your personal situation and needs.

Chapter 8

Preparing for the test

Test preparation is another area where students experience difficulty when it is time to study for Boards. We have strongly emphasized the importance of time management from the beginning of this book. Now is the time when you have to be even more disciplined with time management.

Most students register for the exam between May and July of their second year and spend about four to six uninterrupted weeks studying to prepare for Boards. Believe it or not, that is more than enough time to assimilate all the materials and content you need to know to do well on the exam, assuming you have been very efficient and focused during the school year. Honestly, you might just be wasting your time if you spend more than that. If you think you need more time, you are doing something wrong; most likely you did not plan your time well for studying for the exam.

First and foremost: Please **register early!** Many students procrastinate when it comes to registering early for their exam. Please, we implore you not to be one of those students. You should register as soon as possible to get the best date available.

Rule Number One: Pick a date and ***stick to it!*** We mean it! Pick a date and stick to it. This is very important because you then have a timeline for accomplishing a task. You will begin to work toward completing the task before the time runs out.

Rule Number Two: ***Do not change your exam date!*** We cannot emphasize this enough to students, unless there is an absolute reason to do so. Professional educators have shown that students who change their exam dates do not perform any better on the exam. If you prepare sufficiently, whatever you do not know before your chosen exam date will not change anything.

Rule Number Three: Establish a reasonable and strict time schedule. This is the most important aspect of preparing for your exam. A schedule gives you direction as to how you are doing and helps you anticipate how close you are to accomplishing your goal. There are various options when it comes to making a schedule. You can choose a system-based approach or a basic science approach. A system-based approach focuses on organ systems, cardiology, pulmonary, gastrointestinal, nephrology, et cetera. At the end you can then focus on the basic sciences.

Another approach is focusing on all the basic sciences at the beginning; wrap your studies up with organ systems and weak areas that you need to brush up on. We have included in this section a copy of one of our Board prep schedules for your use. If it works for you, great! If not, it can serve as guide for your personal approach. Every student is different, so we will assume you will do what is best for you.

Chapter 9

Time Schedule for COMLEX and USMLE

As the time passed and we got closer and closer to the Boards, we tried researching online for sample Board schedules that might give us some directions as to how to make our own schedules. We could not find any good source. It was very frustrating, and that is why we have decided to include this chapter in the book.

This is a sample of a seven-week schedule for studying for the Boards, using May 1 through June 14. In order to study effectively, we constructed a fourteen-hour-a-day schedule. The hours are separated into sections and are the same for each day. Fourteen hours might sound a lot, but with frequent breaks and consistent use, you will be accustomed to it by the end of the first week.

There are three blocks in a day that you can allocate for studying. Remember that the average human can only concentrate for forty-five minutes to one hour. Therefore, make it a habit to take ten-minute breaks after every hour of studying. Make sure you take your lunch breaks and use them wisely. Do not prolong your lunch break; make sure you are disciplined with time. When it is 1 pm, it is time to end your break and resume studying.

Exercise is an important aspect of your Board study process. You cannot afford to ignore it. During your second break, go for a run, head to the gym, or play some sport. Your body and brain need exercise to function at maximum capacity.

During the breaks, you can be productive and listen to review lectures or review note cards.

Sleep. Sleep. Sleep. This is extremely crucial to your health during this time. This is not the time to deprive your body of sleep. Make sure you get at least seven to eight hours of good sleep every night. That will refresh your body and improve your memory function as you study. The reason this is crucial is because you want your circadian rhythm to be constant throughout your studying period, allowing you to be refreshed the day before the exam. You do not want to burn out before the day of the test.

Your daily schedule may be similar to the one on the next page.

Daily Time Schedule for COMLEX and USMLE

		TIME	ACTIVITY
1	BLOCK 1 ✓	8 am — 12 pm	STUDY
2	BREAK	12 pm — 1 pm	LUNCH
3	BLOCK 2	1 pm — 5 pm	STUDY ✓
4	BREAK ✓	5 pm — 6 pm	DINNER/EXERCISE
5	BLOCK 3	6 pm — 11 pm	QUESTION BANK ✓
6	BREAK	✓ 11 pm — 7 pm	SLEEPING SLEEP

Note: Your brain needs rest in order to assimilate all the information you have memorized during the day. This is not the time to be staying up all night with coffee in order to read. You need extensive discipline during this time. Try to adhere to your plan as much as possible. We have listed what your typical days over the next weeks will look like. This is a template for you to begin with; it will serve as a guide for your success. Keep in mind, at this stage, the USMLE or COMLEX is about a month to six weeks away. School is over, and you have all day to study for your Boards.

Let us talk about the topics you need to cover and how to allocate time to study for these subjects. These are topics you can find in any Board review books.

GENERAL PRINCIPLES	ORGAN SYSTEMS
Behavioral Science ✓	Cardiovascular
Biochemistry ✓	Endocrine
Embryology ✓	Gastrointestinal
Microbiology ✓	Hematology and Oncology
Immunology ✓	Musculoskeletal and Connective Tissue
Pathology ✓	Neurology
Pharmacology ✓	Psychiatry

We would like to emphasize that this is not a perfect schedule and does not necessarily apply to everyone. It is simply a guide. As you will see, some subjects require more time than others. You might also discover that you cannot complete some organ systems in eight hours of studying *First Aid for the USMLE Step 1*. **Do not panic!** Just postpone the balance till the next day and then complete it, while still following your time schedule.

The key to preparing your day-to-day schedule is to cover the topics in systems using *First Aid for the USMLE Step 1*. At this point, it should be inclusive, containing *all* the information you need, since you have already completed the USMLEWorld Question Bank at least once and possibly some Kaplan questions. You should cover topics like pathology in a system fashion, while topics like biochemistry can be covered on their own.

Here is a sample of a seven-week schedule to help you study for the Boards.

The 7 week schedule

	S	M	T	W	T	F	S
B1	Behavioral science/Ethics	Biochem/Genetic	Biochem	embryo	Micro	Micro	IMMUNO
B2	Behavioral science/Ethics	Biochem/Genetic	Biochem	embryo	Micro	Micro	IMMUNO
B3	UW (50 BS & 50 random questions)	UW (50 Biochemistry & 50 random questions)	UW (50 Biochem & 50 random questions)	UW (50 embryo & 50 random questions)	UW (50 Micro & 50 random qs)	UW (50 Micro & 50 random qs)	UW -50 IMMUNO & 50 RANDOM QS
B1	FA Gen Path	Cardio	Cardio	Endocrine	GI	GI	Heme/Onc
B2	FA Gen pharm	Cardio	Cardio	Endocrine	GI	GI	Heme/Onc
B3	UW RANDOM QS	UW RANDOM QS	UW RANDOM QS	UW RANDOM QS	UW RANDOM QS	UW RANDOM QS	UW RANDOM QS
B1	Heme/Onc	Muscle/CT	Muscle/CT	Neuro/Psych.	Neuro/Psych	Neuro/Psych	Renal
B2	Heme/Onc	Muscle/CT	Muscle/CT	Neuro/Psych.	Neuro/Psych	Neuro/Psych	Renal
B3	UW RANDOM QS	UW RANDOM QS	UW RANDOM QS	UW RANDOM QS	UW RANDOM QS	UW RANDOM QS	UW RANDOM QS

B1: Renal B2 Renal B3: UW RANDOM QS	B1: Repro B2: Repro B3: UW RANDOM QS	B1: Repro B1: Repro B3: UW RANDOM QS	B1: Resp B2: Resp B2: UW RANDOM QS	B1: Resp B2: Resp B3: UW RANDOM QS	Catch up/Rapid Review Wrap up Q's (second time completing the bank)	Catchup Rapid Review Wrap up Q's (second time completing the bank)
USMLE WORLD Self Assessment Exam #1	Review***	Biochem and Genetics Random Q's	Micro and Immuno Random Q's	Micro and Immuno Random Q's	Path and Pharm Random Q's	Cardio Random Q's
Endocrine Random Q's	GI Random Q's	Muscle/CT Random Q's	Heme/Onco Random Q's	Neuro/Psych Random Q's	Neuro/Psych Random Q's	Renal Random Q's
Repro Random Q's	Pulm Random Q's	Rapid Review	USMLE WORLD Self Assesment #2	Review	Review	Review You exam should be arly next week

Key (Abbreviations)

B1: Block 1

B2: Block 2

B3: Block 3

BS: Behavioral science

UW: USMLEWorld → USMLEWorld

Q's: Questions

Biochem: Biochemistry

Heme/Onc: Hematology and Oncology

Micro: Microbiology

Immuno: Immunology

Muscle/CT: Musculoskeletal/connective tissue

Neuro/psch: Neuology and psychiatry

Repro: Reproductive

Resp: Respiratory system

Path: Pathology

Pharm: Pharmacology

Pulm: Pulmonary

Review

Get ready for round two. Rapidly review *First Aid*, one topic per day, starting tomorrow and continue with any questions left over from USMLEWorld or Kaplan or any Qbooks you have.

Important Note: Everyone is different. For some students, going through *First Aid for the USMLE Step 1* the second time may be helpful for reviewing the topics they know they are weak at and need to review one last time. However, other students feel that they are adequately prepared after the first round; they may be concerned about forgetting details as time passes. The decision is ultimately yours; you know yourself best, and you know your strengths and weaknesses. If you plan on going through *First Aid* once, make sure you take the self-assessment exam early in the schedule. Do not take the first assessment exam two days before the exam—bad idea!

How accurate are the assessment exams?

The best and most accurate self-assessment exams are those from USMLEWorld, the NBME website (www.nbme.org), and the Comprehensive Osteopathic Medical Self-Assessment Examination (COMSAE) from the NBOME website (www.nbome.org). NBME and NBOME designed these assessment exams for student practice to give them a sense for what to expect on the actual exam. So you should make wise use of these standardized sample exams.

Their proximity to the real Board exam in terms of grades and difficulty completely depends on when you take them, and how well prepared you are before you sit for them. For example, if you take the self-assessment exam in April before you start your hardcore studying for the Boards, your score will obviously not reflect your potential grade. You may think it is an impossible exam and freak out—for no reason. If, however, you take your assessment exams in June after you have been studying (doing *First Aid* and questions), then your score should reflect what you may get on the actual exam. These self-assessment tests are similar to the MCAT sample exams you practiced before taking the real MCAT (*any memories* ☺). These tests are called self-assessments, because they are supposed to assess your knowledge and preparation for the actual exam.

To summarize, if you want to learn whether you are ready for the real exam, study hard all through and sit for the assessment exam as if you were taking the real exam. At that point, if you do well and you are happy with your score, then proceed and take the exam soon. If you discover that you barely passed with a score you would rather improve, then be happy that you found out early and think carefully about the best next step. You might consider changing the date of your exam; there is nothing wrong with that, because you have a valid reason. It is better to take the COMLEX and USMLE once and do well, than do poorly or fail it and then take it again. Be aware—some residency programs do not accept applicants who failed the COMLEX and/or USMLE, even if they did great the second time.

Chapter 10

Student concerns

Here are some of the common concerns students face when doing practice questions or taking assessment exams:

1. I am very nervous and anxious about the exam.

2. I am not a good standardized test-taker.

3. I always run out of time on standardized exams.

4. The questions are too long.

5. We have to read the question as many times as possible to figure out the answer.

6. We have to answer every question correctly because we are smart and we want to get every question right.

7. I find myself changing exam answers.

Let's look at some solutions for these worrisome concerns and mistakes medical students often make.

1: Test-taker anxiety

Everyone experiences some form of anxiety and stress when it comes to exams. Some have a higher level than of anxiety than others. However, if you could choose one day in your entire life when you want to be the least anxious and worried, it would probably be the CQMLEX or USMLE day—the day for one of the most important exams you will take in your medical career. This is because you only get one shot at it (unless you fail), and if you miss your target, there are no amendments. If you pass the exam, it does not matter if you score 189/75 on the USMLE or 400/75 on the COMLEX; you cannot retake the test ever again, perhaps sad, but true.

There is a difference between stress and anxiety. Anxiety disorder can affect anyone and will negatively influence your studying. This will reflect on your performance during the preparation process and on the actual exam. If you know you have an anxiety disorder, seek help before taking the test. Most schools provide services that help students struggling with anxiety or depression. Those services are there for a reason—use them.

Honestly, no matter how hard you study or how long you study for the exam, you can never be truly satisfied with the level of your preparation for the test. How much work you put into studying prior to your exam date makes the difference. If you have completed two to three thousand questions, you should have no doubt that you are well prepared. And if you have done more questions, then *relax*. Be prepared— it's the best advice we can give you. Anxiety only makes it worse. Allow yourself a relaxed and positive attitude because you have done your best, and accept the fact that you can only prepare so much. Do your part, and leave the rest to God.

2 and 3: I am not a good standardized test-taker *and* I have time issues

Many students use this pair as excuses for poor performance on their Boards, when the real reason was lack of preparation. Consider this: you got through the SATs, undergraduate college exams, the MCAT, graduate school exams (for some of us), and the first two years of medical school, where you took exams every other week. There is no doubt you will make it through this exam, too, unless you work towards failing. Create a different perspective about the test. Think positively about the exam, and realize that you are not the first one to take the test and you will not be the last. When you take the practice tests, time yourself and create an atmosphere to mimic real exam conditions; go to the library or classroom, where you will be less distracted. Practice this way, and you will do well.

4 and 5: Issues with the question style

Remember, there is not much excess time during the exam. Reading each question more than once is wasting time. When you're doing practice questions or taking assessment exams, you should aim at reading each question once and only once. Read it slowly and carefully. Every word counts but be careful! Words can count for you and against you. How? Many of the questions as you will see in USMLEWorld and Kaplan question banks include extra information put there to distract you and widen your differential. Try to stay focused and read the question without distractions. If you have read it carefully and still cannot answer the questions, chances are that you simply do not know the answer. Mark it and return to it if you have time at the end of the block. *Do not* panic. Maybe you are overthinking it; maybe it is just a topic you never studied. Move on to score points from questions you *can* answer.

What works for many people is to first read the question statement (usually the last sentence of the question paragraph). This helps you select the relevant clues from the question paragraph and identify the key that opens the answer.

Many questions can be answered based on the information given combined with a little or sometimes no information beyond the question. You need to read such questions in detail.

Example: "Blah BlahBlah. What is the most likely diagnosis?"

or

"Blah BlahBlah. What is the most likely cause of this disease?"

With these types of questions, read the whole paragraph and use every hint to rule in and rule out possible answers.

However, some questions describe the disease, tell you what it is, and then ask you something else about it. This completely depends on your knowledge of the fact that the specific question is addressing. Basically, you could have just read the last sentence and answered the question. In that case, reading the whole paragraph wasted time; you could have just skipped to the last sentence and answered the question.

Example. "Blah BlahBlah. The patient was diagnosed with Duchene Muscular Dystrophy. What is the mode of inheritance of this disease?"

Answer: Autosomal dominant.

The point is clear—save time when you can, read quickly but efficiently, and do not let them trick you with extra information.

6. Answering all the questions correctly

Answering all the questions correctly is impossible, simply because these exams test material from many books, and there is no way you can cover everything for the exam. Study hard, do your best, and aim for the best scores, but be realistic. Deciding in advance that you must answer each question correctly will do nothing but hurt you, because every time you can't answer a question, it increases your anxiety and nurtures a pessimistic attitude.

The worst feeling is missing the easy questions, the stuff you felt silly reviewing because you knew it better than your name before you sat for the exam. Now under the influence of anxiety, it completely flies out of your head, and you sit there biting your fingers and hitting your head on the desk. Stop! Move on, and come back to it later. There is a high chance that you will remember the answer in a few minutes, when you are less anxious.

Please do not take any books (especially your *First Aid* book) with you to the testing center. As soon as you walk out for every break, you are going to check your answers—you know it! Do not do that.

Do not read your *First Aid* during break sessions either! Take the time to relax and walk around the center to get fresh air. The exam is long and requires a positive attitude and rested mind the entire time. Do not get your mind busy with negative thoughts about how or why you missed that one question. It is okay; it is okay; it is okay. It happens to everyone.

7. Changing exam answers

This is a huge no-no during the exam. The probability that you will change the right answer to a wrong one is very high, about 85 percent (confirmed by personal experience!). Warning! Warning! Except if you are *absolutely* sure that you chose the wrong answer initially, please, *do not change your first answer.* Do you know why they call the wrong answers *distractors*? Because they are wrong; do not fall for them.

Make it a habit, even when you do practice questions, to pick one answer and move on. If you are not sure, mark it and go back if you have extra time. Do not waste your time looking through the answers if you know the right answer. You are almost certainly correct. Leave your answer alone and move on. Trust us—on the actual exam, you will still be tempted to do this! It is almost inevitable, but try your best to avoid this urge.

For example: "A twenty-eight-week primigravida woman presents with painless vaginal bleeding …"The answer is placenta previa! Do not waste your time with other options; move on!

After the Test

It is important to correlate the feelings and emotions you experience after taking the assessment exams to the scores you get on the assessment exams. The reason we say that is because you will walk out of the actual test feeling very similarly to how you felt after the assessment exam, and that should tell you how you did on the test. Hopefully it should be good news for you.

For example, after taking every single assessment exam, we felt horrible afterwards and thought that we failed. However, the scores were really good. Some of our friends felt that they did really well and ended up getting similar scores to us. On the day of the actual exams, we walked out thinking we failed, while some of our friends walked out thinking they did awesome. It felt just like taking another self-assessment exam, except that we did not get the scores right away. But it was comforting to know that we felt the same way as we did when we were taking our assessment exams, and we probably had done just as well.

Celebrate regardless! No matter how bad you think you did, still celebrate, because you deserve it. You just completed one of the most difficult exams in your life. Most likely, you got the score you expected based on your assessment exams. It takes about four weeks to receive the USMLE scores and six weeks to receive the COMLEX scores. NBME will send an e-mail the morning of the day the scores are to be released, and the scores will be available online. You can print it for up to 120 days. The report includes a three-digit score, the two-digit score, and a breakdown of the topics (pathology, anatomy, et cetera). NBOME will mail a letter with the score report of your COMLEX exam, similar to the USMLE report, and scores will also be available online. Regardless of your scores, keep a positive attitude and be flexible and smart about your choices when it comes to residency.

Chapter 11

Advice for osteopathic students

The Dilemma

The dilemma that DO students face is "Do I need to take the USMLE?"

The answer to this question is simple, yet complicated at the same time. It really depends on the student first and foremost. There are two answers to this question, and of course they contradict each other. One point of view is, why take another difficult test if you are not planning to go to a competitive allopathic residency? Most allopathic programs accept the COMLEX scores anyways. Also, taking the USMLE is more work and stress than simply taking the COMLEX alone, so why bother to pay the extra $500 and go through more torture? Some people agree with this view, and others look at it as taking the easy way out.

The other point of view focuses on applying for highly competitive specialties: Emergency medicine, radiology, ophthalmology, anesthesia, dermatology, and surgery (known by the widely recognized mnemonic EROADS) residencies. Surgical specialties include neurosurgery, urology, and ear nose and throat (ENT). These residencies are very difficult to obtain. The program directors receive a wide range of excellent applicants with great scores for a limited number of spots. The highly competitive pool of applicants forces the program directors to establish a minimum Board score for selecting the students to interview. Therefore, taking the USMLE can open more doors, since it is a very solid way for the residency directors of allopathic programs to compare you to your fellow MD applicants. Many Accreditation Council for Graduate Medical Education (ACGME) program directors may feel more comfortable looking at USMLE scores because it is a good way to compare you to the rest of the applicants.

However, just as taking the USMLE step 1 exam can open doors for you as an osteopathic student; it can also close doors to your application too. If you fail or barely pass the USMLE exam, it will count against you and hurt your application rather than help it.

Therefore, the decision is ultimately personal. Just realize that signing up for the USMLE has its pros and cons, but it is definitely more work—a lot more work, as you will find out as you begin your journey—than just taking the COMLEX. The best thing to do if you are seriously thinking about taking the USMLE is to actually make up your mind and decide *early*. The sooner the better, because you need to realize the amount of extra work you will need to put in. Begin the process of preparing early. If you decide to take both Board exams, you have to fully understand the repercussions of your decision. It demands twice the amount of work.

Our personal point of view is that you have already assumed more than $100,000 in loans; what is an extra $500? Especially if you do not know what field of medicine you are going into. What if you end up falling in love with anesthesia, urology, radiology, or ear, nose, and throat (ENT)? Unfortunately, there are not enough osteopathic residencies, and those are all competitive residencies, so you need your application to stand out. Or what if you realize that you want to be in a certain geographical area (for whatever reason: family, spouse, city, life) where there are no osteopathic residencies? Then your only route is applying to an allopathic residency. Personally, we were not sure what we wanted to specialize in, and we wanted to have all the doors open and all options available; hence we took both exams. **It is crucial to know what you are signing up for, though, when you decide to take the USMLE on top of the COMLEX, as emphasized before.**

The biggest mistake DO students make is "giving the USMLE a shot." The USMLE deserves more than just a shot. It is a beast, if we are generous in describing this test. The exam is now a worldwide gold standard for all applicants interested in an ACGME residency. It is a very challenging exam, and you must be mentally prepared for it.

Although MD students dread taking the USMLE, they take it once and they run! In the meantime, you as a DO student may accept the challenge of sitting for the eight-hour long exam. Then you return home to continue to study again for the COMLEX. This can either make or break you, because you do not have time to process whether you did well or not on the USMLE. You still have to anticipate sitting for the COMLEX and doing well on it. We say this not to scare you, but just to give you a dose of reality. Remember, *you must pass your COMLEX regardless of how well you perform on the USMLE.* It is a graduation requirement - to pass COMLEX-USA Level 1, 2 Comlex Exam and Performance Examination (PE).

As an osteopathic student, your main exam is COMLEX, and your priority is to do well on your COMLEX. If you make the choice to sign up for both exams, you need to find the balance to do well on both. Some osteopathic medical students who take the USMLE do not perform as well on the COMLEX because they studied for both exams using the USMLE question bank and *First Aid for the USMLE* and then added the Osteopathic Manipulative Medicine (OMM) portion of COMLEX to the end of their preparation for COMLEX. *This method may not work.* As we mentioned before, the exams are different and require different approaches to tackle the questions. We highly recommend the Kaplan COMLEX question bank and COMBANK to study for COMLEX. Also, you have to study OMM continuously and not leave it until the last few days after the USMLE exam, immediately prior to COMLEX.

The best way to determine if you have a chance of doing well on the USMLE test is to take one of the NBME sample assessment exams online under standardized conditions; whatever score you receive will predict your actual performance on the real exam. So, if you take the USMLE assessment test and do not do well, re-think your decision about the exam. A poor score will hurt your application and might count against you.

Osteopathic residency directors do not care about your USMLE score, but if you apply to an allopathic residency, there is no way to hide it. In the case of a poor USMLE score, you would have been better off not taking the USMLE, because the allopathic residency director would have had only your COMLEX scores on hand.

Also, a common scenario is the students who realized in their third year that "oops, I probably should have taken the USMLE." Such students are in a very stressful situation, feeling regret and anxiety as they decide what to do next. We know that third year is *not* a vacation, as many people make it seem. It is an energy-depriving year, and you have COMLEX-Level

II USA and COMLEX Physical Exam (PE) to complete at the end of the fourth year. It is hard enough to study for the rotation you are on after a long day of work. (We promise you will miss the first and second years, when you had lectures and went home to review them.) Going to rotations is like going to work, usually from 7am to 5pm, or longer if you are on surgery rotation. Imagine adding the stress of preparing for USMLE step 1 in the third year—it is tough. It is not going to be easy to study for such a big exam in the midst of studying for shelf exams and Step II exams. Therefore, decide *early* and start preparing *early*—in your second year, not during third year.

If you are planning on taking the USMLE exam, you need to put in 100 percent effort and aim for a strong score. It is not to be taken lightly; it is a serious decision you have to make, preferably early on in your second year. If you sign up for it, put in the hours, studying smart to excel on this exam. If you decide not to take it, just hope that the allopathic residency program you apply to accept COMLEX scores only.

You must report your USMLE scores if you are applying to any ACGME programs. From the **Electronic Residency Application Service (ERAS)** instructions:

"**Note to osteopathic applicants only:** Before you certify your ERAS application, consider whether you will apply to ACGME and/or American Osteopathic Association (AOA) accredited programs. If you apply to ACGME accredited programs and you have taken the USMLE, you must report that on your common applications (CAF). If you only apply to AOA accredited programs, you do not have to report the USMLE on your common application form (CAF)." Read more on the American

Osteopathic Association website. http://www.osteopathic.org/inside-aoa/
Education/ed-center/Pages/electronic-residency-application-service.aspx

Obviously, some students do not need to take the USMLE and do not
have to worry about making this decision:

1. Students who know for a fact they want to practice osteopathic
    manipulative medicine (OMM).

2. Students who want to stay in a system within their osteopathic
    university hospital.

3. Students who do not want to apply to competitive allopathic
    residencies.

4. DO students applying to less competitive residencies or residencies
    that have a large portion of DO students.

Do not listen to anyone who tries to convince you to the take the
USMLE just to prove your intelligence. The choice is yours. Some students
say they wanted to satisfy their ego; that is why they wanted to take the
USMLE. But this is not a good reason at all. Other motivational factors
should drive you to take the USMLE. Satisfying your ego is simply not
enough reason to take such an exam; it can count against you if you do
not receive a high score. You need to set a goal; say to yourself that you
need to take the USMLE for reasons a, b, and c, and on top of that you
will show all the allopathic residency directors that you can do just as well
on their exam. This should be the attitude.

USMLE Recommendations for Osteopathic Students *Only*

These are some reasons you should *not* take the USMLE if you are an
osteopathic medical student.

1. I want to satisfy my ego.

2. I want to show my other MD friends I can do what they can do,
    or even better.

3. I want to impress my parents and friends because I sat for two
    Board exams.

4. I just want to take it for the fun of it, to get a feel for what the exam is like.

5. I did not do well on my USMLE assessment test a week before the test. (That is an alarming sign—pay attention.)

6. I am still scoring less than 50 percent on my USMLEWorld or Kaplan question bank in the last week before the exam.

7. I just want to take the exam to pass the test; my score is not important because I am only applying to osteopathic residencies any way.

Comparing the USMLE and COMLEX

Realize that the USMLE and COMLEX are two different exams and will obviously have two different styles. The best way for students to see the difference is to go to the NBOME and NBME websites and take a look at the sample questions posted, as well as question formats and styles on their website. The links have been provided below.

For USMLE sample questions, refer to the NBME website: USMLE Step 1 Question Format: http://www.usmle.org/Examinations/step1/step1_test.html

USMLE Step 1 Content Description online: http://www.usmle.org/Examinations/step1/step1_content.html

For COMLEX style sample question, refer to the NBOME website: NBOME COMSAE sample question format: http://www.nbome.org/comsae-boi.asp?m=can#format

COMLEX Level Content Description online: http://www.nbome.org/comsae-boi.asp?m=can#content2

For more information about the COMLEX Level I, III and III. Visit www.nbome.org.

As you can see, the styles of the exams are quite different from each other, and doing well on both exams requires you to be able to handle different types of questions. That requires a decent amount of work and effort. Handling both exams is possible, but it must be done in a careful manner to avoid overwhelming yourself and failing both exams. The last thing you need is to do poorly on both exams because you could not manage 100 percent effort on both and settled for 80 percent effort. If you ever feel that you are in that position and an exam date is coming up, then maybe you are better off forfeiting the $500 and not sitting for the USMLE. Instead, spend the last few days focusing on the COMLEX. Again, judge your progress by your performance on the assessment exams.

One student may tell you he had more biochemistry on his exam, while another student will tell you she had more neurology on her exam. Please do not listen to anyone who shares such information because they are misleading you. First of all, they should not be discussing the content of the exam, as this violates the terms and conditions of the exam. Secondly, every student's exam is different and the content of the test varies from one examinee to another. You should study everything you can; prepare for any question that might be posed to you on the actual exam.

Please do not forget to study epidemiology and behavioral sciences for both exams; many students push these topics to the end or do not even bother studying them at all. Be careful not to fall into that trap.

Finally, most osteopathic students who take both exams take the USMLE before the COMLEX. The biggest mistake they fall into is scheduling the two exams three days apart. This is not the smartest idea, because you need to physically and emotionally recover from the first test. You need a mental break and you need more time to prepare for the transition between the two exam styles. If you decide to take both, you need to start preparing for both early and equally. That means studying questions from COMBANK and USMLEWorld together. You should schedule at least seven to ten days between them before you sit for the COMLEX in order to recover from the first exam, get over any emotions, and focus more on last-minute high-yield material that pertains to the second exam. What most people do is take the USMLE first, and then take the COMLEX, and focus on OMM in the seven to ten days in between. That being said, everyone is different. You might want to leave fewer or more days for whatever reason; again, do what you think is best for you. **Just remember, the USMLE Step 1 and COMLEX Level 1 are two different exams and require different preparations.**

Chapter 12

Summary chapter for Board review

1. Plan your COMLEX/USMLE review schedule by looking at the big picture. Estimate how many hours your total review will involve. How many days do you have? How many hours are in a (realistic) study day? Take out a calendar and count the hours available, being conservative. If you divide this total by seven (the number of basic science subjects), it gives you a rough average of the time available per subject. Adjust these time frames around your strong/weak areas.

2. Decide if your study will be organized by subjects or by organ systems. The COMLEX/USMLE questions are written from the "integrated" point of view and that integrated framework is from your pre-clinical knowledge; however, your books and notes have not always packaged the information in that form. Sequence the topics ahead of time so you have a good framework and use questions from different "subjects" in close time proximity to help make your thinking more interdisciplinary.

3. Determine your order of topics. One school of thought is to study weak areas first, as they eat up more time. For example, spend more time on topics such as microbiology and biochemistry (for both COMLEX and USMLE). These topics require lots of

memorization, and you might need between two to three days to study for these. Refer back to the sample schedule (chapter 9). The other method concentrates on reviewing "easier" material first. Use the rest of the time to focus on more challenging topics. However, you know which topics need to be studied or reviewed near the end of your preparation because they are quickly forgotten. Consider how to coordinate the study of related topics, e.g. renal physiology on the same day(s) as renal pathology, etc. This is essential to learning materials conceptually rather than in isolation. Determine whether you will study one subject fully before switching, or, better yet, integrate the material.

4. Avoid alcohol and drugs. Do not laugh, this is actually serious. Some students abuse these substances.

5. You cannot perform well if you are depressed—do not take the test; take a leave of absence and seek help through your school or other places where you can receive adequate treatment.

6. Select review sources for all topics before you begin; switch sources only for a good reason. Do not let panic drive you to exceed the time and material you had scheduled for a given topic. From the beginning, put **practice question time** on your study schedule. Use them to 1) preview a topic, 2) test knowledge of a topic, and 3) refresh your memory on a topic. Periodic comprehensive exams, which help you practice switching from topic to topic, are also good training, but save these for later in the schedule.

7. Regular routine build confidence in your progress. Eat well, sleep well, exercise, and protect yourself from negative influences. Take care of yourself like an athlete in training. This COMLEX/USMLE immersion study experience can improve your discipline.

8. Use study groups and partners if they have the right pace and approach for your needs. Coordinate the topics, plan in advance and prepare for the sessions.

9. Does anxiety hinder either your study or your test-taking? The good antidote is to do practice questions and habitually analyze your

errors. See if you are capable of predicting your own performance. If anxiety or other factors affect your progress, ask for help in your school or wherever you can receive adequate treatment. They should offer services for students who are having anxiety issues.

Five Principles for Effective Learning and Test-Taking

- *Keep learning active.* Whether you learn best by preparing written summaries, reciting information aloud, or making diagrams or concept maps, do whatever it takes to *learn it the first time*! This will make your study process much more efficient, since you can spend more time reviewing—which is critical to *retaining* information.

- *"Encode" the information in as many ways as possible.* This is how you can make learning an active process, by making *meaning* from the material, connecting it to other facts you already know, using mnemonics, sound effects, YouTube, colorful analogies, or metaphors and by categorizing the information in a meaningful way; e.g., the top three diseases among women, the five cities where a particular microbe is found (Histoplasmosis, Blastomycosis, Coccidiomycosis). Also, incorporating all the senses is best for recall.

- *Attempt to visualize information.* The latest research into long-term memory shows that we store and recall information in terms of images, events, and experiences. So any method you can use to make an image more vivid—e.g., making it multisensory, using color coding—will make facts easier to recall.

- *Repeat reviews.* This is what ultimately shifts information from short- to long-term memory and maintains retention. **Active learning + regular reviews = long-term retention**. If any one part of this equation is missing, you risk not really knowing and recalling the information when needed.

- *Practice testing.* Use this method of error correction to determine where you need to focus your study time. Continually assess what you've learned, go over your errors, and clarify any unclear concepts.

Question Analysis Duringthe *Study Process*→Three Steps

1. ***Identify topics.*** Identify all possible topics that are being covered by the question and the answer choices. Highlight or circle *all* the words that could possible change the meaning.

2. ***Understand the correct answer ...for obvious reasons!***

3. ***Understand the wrong answers and why they're wrong.*** Incorrect answers are plausible or they would not be good distractors. For this reason, it's extremely valuable to go over the wrong answers as well. Ask yourself: "under what circumstances would this answer be correct?" By doing so, you learn *four times* as much about the topic, you learn better test-taking skills, and you also uncover the pattern and subtleties of question construction. Going through this process can prepare you for other questions!

Question AnalysisDuringthe *Exam*→Five Steps

1. ***Identify topics.*** Identify all possible topics that are being covered by the question and the answer choices. Highlight or circle them.

2. ***Try to answer the question intuitively first.*** See if you can guess at the answer before looking at the choices. This will give you some indication of what your intuition tells you.

3. ***Rephrase the question*** to clarify the meaning. Make changes in the answer choices to make them correct.

4. ***Use the "differential diagnosis" approach*** to eliminate as many choices as possible.

5. ***Do a "K-check"*** (kinesthetic check) if you are still unable to guess at the correct answer. Rely on your intuition. If you feel pretty confident about an answer, do not try to convince yourself otherwise!

During the exam, *do not* ...

- Let yourself get mentally down after the first day. Most Board exams are failed on the second day because people mentally let down. Be sure to keep yourself sharp until the very end.

- Try to determine how well you are doing. You won't be able to be objective, and you'll only increase your anxiety.

- Expect to feel like a "master of the medical universe." Chances are that you will probably not achieve the level of competency you are used to. Remember, this is a nationally standardized exam—not a mastery test.

We hope this summarizes your approach to Board studying.

Chapter 13

Surviving medical school

Although this book was written to provide you the secrets and "ins and outs" of how to dissect the Bible of medical school, the *First Aid for the USMLE Step 1* review book, and how to master your Boards, this short chapter is designed to give you some tips and basic rules that you should always keep in mind throughout your journey as a medical student. It is all about studying smart and studying hard. Notice: studying smart comes before studying hard, because time is the most invaluable treasure and your closest friend during medical school. If you can manage your time successfully, you can still enjoy your life to a certain extent (do not get too excited). We put this chapter at the end of the book because we did not want to deviate from the big picture of the book, which, in a nut shell, is studying effectively for the Boards.

The following are the most common "big" mistakes that students commit from day one in medical school. Unfortunately, many students eventually realize that they caused more damage than good to their minds and bodies. Some of these damages are short-term, while others are long-term. For example, students experience quick burnout after their first year of medical school due to intense and continuous studying. Many students sacrifice their health for medical school. Imagine your cholesterol level at 250 mg/dl from all the hamburgers and free pizzas that you ate at the club meetings or presentations you attended. This is all avoidable; at least recognize what the mistakes are, so you can minimize the damage early on.

The rule is simple; you do not need to sacrifice much besides time to get through medical school. Sacrificing other things, like your health, should be a warning sign to you that you are not being efficient with your time. So read the following carefully …

Number Zero: Realizing what you got yourself into

The study of medicine is a long process and demands a great amount of discipline and sacrifice. Yet the reward is priceless. Many physicians say that it is not the same as it used to be, that things have changed quite a bit. Although this might be true, they are strictly talking about money. The financial reward might have decreased, but as a first-year or second-year student, you should not be thinking about medicine only in terms of money. We are hoping that you picked medicine for the amazing field that it is, the rich opportunities it provides for helping humans, and the avenues it opens for making a difference in the world. Think of the bright side—you will be providing people with medical care and a better life until you decide to retire; something as simple as giving sample medication to someone whose co-pay is high can ease the suffering of that patient. So think of every long night of studying as an opportunity to learn to become a great physician one day. Think of all the people who did not get into medical school who wish they were in your spot.

Medicine is rewarding in many aspects besides money, and it will all come once you graduate and finish residency. So be patient—the path of medical school is long, but it has an end, a bright and happy one. Yet this end is the beginning of another journey, where you harvest the products of your hard work and continue getting rewards on a daily basis with every patient you help as a practicing physician.

Number One: Depriving yourself of healthy, fresh food and buying fast food, junk, and processed foods

This very common and very serious mistake is usually committed for the sake of saving time to study. Imagine what you put your body through, just so you can gain an extra ten or fifteen minutes for studying. Over a two-year period, there might be long-term consequences to your health. Your brain needs fresh food, water, fruits, and vegetables. Please try to graduate medical school without ulcers, hypertension, diabetes, and high cholesterol. There is no reason you should not be able to cook (if you know how to) or buy veggies and fruits. Your brain works better on bananas and

Health Save — handwritten annotation

fresh - Fruits, Vegetables, milk, Banana Save — handwritten annotation

strawberries than on French fries and popcorn. We guarantee you, not only will you save money, but you will save something far more important— your health from deteriorating.

Number Two: Ruining your health by not exercising

"Oh, why should I waste thirty minutes on exercise when I can read a few more pages about the obesity, heart attacks, and strokes that happen to people with sedentary life styles?" Sounds like a contradiction to anyone?

Again, this is a very common mistake, and it affects more students than those who used to avidly work out and exercise before medical school started. You will be sad, with low self-esteem and less energy than you can potentially experience if you do exercise. You should be able to maintain at least a thirty-minute workout four times a week up until the day of your Boards. It is not wasted time; you can listen to lectures at the same time and hit two birds with one stone. Your body deserves to stay healthy and be in a great shape. Work exercise into your schedule; make it a mandatory part of your day. Most medical schools have a gym on campus, which should be sufficient for a quick thirty-minute power workout—so no excuses.

Number Three: Pulling all-nighters and depriving your body and brain of sleep

Neglecting sleep is such a bad idea. As grandma says, healthy body, healthy mind. We guarantee you if you pull an all-nighter and go to class the next day: one, you will not absorb much; two, you will be wasting time because you will probably end up having to listen to the lecture again; and three, you will probably need a nap when you come back from school, which means you will sleep later and wake up the next day sleep-deprived … and the cycle continues. If you plan your time well, you should be able to get the seven or eight hours that you were used to before medical school. Your classmates may hate you, because their sleep cycles will be all messed up, and they'll be exhausted all the time. But that's okay; it is about being smart with your time.

Caffeine addiction is common among medical students. Beware of this! Not only will you develop side effects and withdrawal symptoms, it might reflect negatively on your studies. Caffeine might wake you up the night before the test, but it might not get you through the test. We cannot tell you not to drink coffee, but everything should be in moderation. **Needless to say, please stay away from alcohol and drugs!**

Number Four: Competing with your classmates and comparing your grades with others

We are all know we had to be competitive to get into the field of medicine. By now, we believe you are aware of that. However, medical school is a leveling ground for all of us. We all came from various backgrounds and different undergraduate schools, where enduring the pressure of getting good grades to enter medical school was about the survival of the fittest.

But once you are accepted to medical school, it becomes a level plain field, where the better of the best students are assembled to learn medicine.

Most medical students are still engulfed in the mentality of competing with other students, for numerous reasons: satisfaction, to measure their progress, a superiority complex, or because it simply feels good. These attributes will clearly not make you a better physician, and because you score a 95 percent on your pathology exam has no bearing on whether you will be a great pathologist or clinician.

As soon as you walk out of your first exam, look around. You will see people screaming at each other, pulling their hair, and gambling their lives away on what answer was right for question number thirteen. It is easy to spot them; they will ask you if you chose option C for question 84. Seriously? Do they think you'll remember that? Avoid everyone after the exam, and be friends with those who share this philosophy, because the moment the exam is over, you should be ready to move on to the next task. When the grade is released, you can review the test on your own and see where your mistakes are so you can avoid them in the future. The best advice we received during our career as undergraduate students was from an organic chemistry teacher, Dr. Maria Vogt, PhD, from Bloomfield College, who warned us, "You love to compete with other students because you make them your yard stick for measuring your progress and how smart you think you are, but what you do not know is that there are a lot of smarter people than you out there. The best way to be your best is to compete only with yourself, because you will never out compete yourself, and you will become a better person every time you try again."

We listened to this advice, and we can testify that it helped us tremendously to succeed in medical school. We never wanted to know what people's grades were; neither did we discuss exam questions or share grades with others. Comparing grades will create a hostile competitive environment that is absolutely unnecessary; you need to be with people who are calm and happy and not bragging about their 93 percent on the physiology quiz.

Number Five: Spending time with negative people

It is easy to spot them. They walk around looking angry, depressed, and constipated. They always talk about how they hate their lives, and they regret getting into medical school because they never sleep enough. School is too hard; they do not have time to go to the gym, et cetera. Their Facebook status is updated at least three times a day with derogative statements about medical school. Stay away from such students, because they will drag you into their pessimism and convert you into one of the miserable people. Instead, be a positive person. Smile! You are lucky you got into medical school; why aren't you thankful?

Most medical schools in the United States accept one to two hundred applicants out of five to six thousand. Day by day, it is getting more difficult to get into medical school, and many people wish they had your spot. No one said it would be easy, but success is definitely achievable. You should appreciate the gift of being a medical student—be happy that your journey began. Although it is hard now, it will get better after you take your Boards and start clinical rotations.

Number Six: "Studying my notes ten times is probably the best way to prepare for exams."

Wrong! Do questions from day one. The only way to test your learning is to do questions. For example, after studying your BRS physiology text book, make sure you complete the questions at the end of each chapter. This will help solidify the concepts you just read. **Studying the same thing over and over does not make you smarter, but getting a question**

wrong will teach you quite a bit. Even regarding the Boards, professional educators will tell you that it is statistically proven that students who do more questions perform better on Boards, and that the only time you should go back to the big books is when you consistently miss questions on a certain topic and find that the explanations from the questions are not doing the job.

Number Seven: "I will study for the Boards in March before my exam in June."

Not a very good idea. People will tell you that their fifth cousin did that and got 260 on USMLE or 740 on COMLEX. Please do not believe them—unless NBME sent them the wrong report, it is impossible to get such a score without hard work. Studying for the Boards begins day one of medical school. Preparing is a tough process that only a few people complete in the correct fashion. We think we've made this point very clear throughout the book.

Number Eight: "Studying ten books on one subject is the best way to cover all the possible material they might test on the Boards."

The fact is you will never know it all, and it is impossible to predict what new topics the Board questions will cover. The high-yield material is in the review books, but even the review books will not have it all. That being said, pick a good review book that students' reviews recommend. Reading an entire pathology text before the Boards is probably not the smartest idea, but you can use one as a reference. Stick to one book you like for each subject, and do questions, the more the merrier. Again, use *Fist Aid for the USMLE Step 1* wisely.

Number Nine: "I am going to be a machine and memorize it all, just memorize, memorize, memorize."

Depending on your school and the curriculum it follows, you will start your first day in school with some level of biochemistry, anatomy, physiology, histology, et cetera. On day one, columnar cells, impulse transmission, and glycolysis are probably covered. The next day, you learn about brachial plexus

77

and cardiac output. This is an enormous amount of information overload, and students are often not prepared for it, so we all memorize, right?

Let us share a short story with you. Being told that we'd better be memorizing machines, we got our coffee, Red Bull, and power snacks and started memorizing like there was no tomorrow. Even on day one, we said to ourselves we were going to memorize the book from cover to cover, including the ISBN number and the author's name. We memorized a tremendous amount of information. After talking to some people the next day, we realized, however, that we only retained about 50 percent of the material, and that we did not really have a solid understanding of what was going on. We realized that we packed the info in little Ziplock bags in our brains; it was all isolated—nothing was integrated. Biochemistry notes about diabetes were just biochemistry notes to us; we did not know how we could possibly link it to physiology, and we blamed it on the school curriculum, which of course is not true. We did not have the big picture in mind. Big picture?

If the material is not integrated in your mind and organized for your understanding, you will not retain the information in your long-term memory. More details will be discussed later, but the main idea is to think of medical school as one class; it is your job to integrate it all and make it flow.

Number Ten: "I cannot wait to be done with the Boards so I can forget all this useless information."

Oh, you did *not* just say that, did you? You will be surprised that most of what you learn in the first two years of medical school will return during residency. Attending physicians and residents like to pimp on material they are comfortable with. Some of them like microbiology, and they will make your life miserable if you do not know your bugs, while others like pharmacology and will torture you if you do not know your drugs. One day you may be doing rounds with a GI fellow who knows everything about the GI system—yes, everything, including histology, anatomy, and physiology. The next day you are with the endocrine doctor who loves hormones. Notice, this is what you learned in the first two years. So learn the material; do not just memorize it. Know it for life. **The best way to evaluate your understanding of a topic is your ability to explain it to others**; if you can do that, then you learned it well.

Number Eleven: "I am going to study on my own because I do not need anyone's help."

Medicine is all about teamwork and sharing information. You have to be able to cooperate and work with others in groups. Even when you apply for residency, it is very important to keep this concept in mind. The moment the medical team feel that you will not be a good team player and you may have "issues" with your colleagues in the hospital is the moment your application goes in the shredder.

Although it may be true, that you *can* study on your own, it will benefit you to find yourself a small group of people (two or three maximum) who share the same principles—they like to exercise, do not like to share grades, and have a positive attitude. Once you find the right group of people, arrange to meet for two or three hours weekly for a very efficient session. Ask each other questions about concepts you do not understand, or even better, "pimp" each other on little details you think your friends might have understood. Also, arrange for a review session the night before the exam for last minute "pimping." It works great. We cannot tell you how many times friends pimped us on stuff that we didn't know, even things we had underlined six times and highlighted seven times but still did not know. Most importantly, have a clique leader to keep people on track if the topics being discussed shift from glycolysis to football or shoes. The group leader should be the most anxious of you all, the one who is always stressed out and shaking his or her leg.

Number Twelve: "I do not have time to study for the physiology quiz. Let me just do last year's exam—I heard they repeat questions."

Although it is important to do questions, it is more important to do them after you learn the material. Many people try to take the easy way out and just memorize the answers to questions from last year's material instead of studying. Please do not do it. All the material is on the Boards, and anything you do not study now is something extra you have to study for before the Boards. Do not procrastinate! Use your time efficiently to avoid this situation; study and then do questions. **Remember, studying for physiology is studying for the Boards! Learn it now.**

Number Thirteen: "I am so stressed out."

Stress is normal; everyone in your class is facing similar amounts of stress, some more than others. But you will notice some people walking around with a frown on their face, while some wear a huge smile. How is that difference possible, if they are all in the same class, under the same pressure? The key is time. If you have some extra time, you are able to reduce stress. First, your friends will play a very important role—that's what friends are for, especially if they are your classmates. They can help you calm down when you are freaking out. Secondly, do something on your own that makes you feel better, whether that is exercise, yoga, listening to calm music, talking to your parents, or praying, something out there that makes you feel better. Find it and do it. Do not let the stress affect your studies, relationships, or, most importantly, health. No one said medical school was easy; it is very stressful and demanding. However, managing stress will become very important; otherwise you will realize it is taking a toll on your life.

To Recap ...

You are going to be a doctor—step up to the prestige of the profession. Think of yourself as two entities, your body and your brain. Your brain needs to be happy in order for you to succeed in medical school. Therefore, eat healthy, exercise, sleep enough, keep your grades to yourself, stay positive and avoid negative people, study smart from day one, do questions, and study for the Boards as early as possible. Get the big picture of any topic you are covering and relate it back to the Boards. Notice all the items above share one common factor: *time*. We think time is very sacred and that it deserves a discussion here.

We all agree that managing your time is the key factor to success in medical school. So how do you study in an efficient way and make time for other activities besides studying? Everyone studies differently, but find a way that works for you, and keep adjusting it as you go along to perfect it. You will know you are doing the right thing when you have time for yourself outside of studying. Yes, it is possible to find extra time for non-school activities, such as exercise, a social life, piano, soccer ... whatever you like to do, you can do it. The key points are to always plan ahead, always make a schedule, and stick to it. Studying smart, as mentioned earlier, includes studying the right material in a way so that you retain it in the shortest amount of time. For some people, this may mean talking out loud; others write on a whiteboard or make note cards; others draw, and others just read. Try all the methods and stick to your chosen method. Our clique was like a mafia; people in school knew we were walking dynamos. We were efficient to the point that we always managed to end our review session around 11pm the night before the test and still get our eight hours of sleep. We excelled on the exams. Looking at other people who studied all night, it was very obvious that what they were doing was wrong, and there was no reason why they needed to deprive themselves of sleep to survive medical school.

Finally, we cannot emphasize this enough, we are all in a great profession. Be passionate about what you are learning! Medicine is a treasure, medicine is an art. As Henri Amiel said:

"To me the ideal doctor would be a man endowed with profound knowledge of life and of the soul, intuitively divining any suffering or disorder of whatever kind, and restoring peace by his mere presence."

Thank you for purchasing this book. We invite you to visit our website www.ftpinc.org for videos on different topics that can help you study for Boards.

~Adeleke and Farook

From the authors to our beloved reader:

We hope this book has been an invaluable tool to you as a reader, and that the contents have shed some light on how to prepare for the Board examinations and survive medical school. We understand your concerns and are fully aware of how deeply you want to succeed, simply because we were once in your shoes.

Your ability to succeed in life depends on how much effort you are willing to invest. Like everyone else, you have the potential to do whatever you set your mind to do. You also possess the key to your potential freedom and success. You are the captain of your own ship, and you certainly have an influence on your destiny as an individual. We implore you to maintain a positive attitude throughout this process and focus on your goal.

It is important for you to know that one of life's lesson is, "Success does not go to those who are have a genius and a natural talent for knowledge, but to those who are willing to put enough time and work to realize their goal." ~Anonymous~

In conclusion, "There are no secrets to success. It is the result of perseverance, hard work, and learning from failure."- Colin Powel

We wish you all the best on your exams. Good luck!

Chapter 14

Resources

The following are high-yield, A+ rated resources that are recommended by students who took the USMLE and COMLEX.

Review Courses

Kaplan Medical Review Coursehttp://www.kaptest.com/Medical-Licensing/USMLE-Prep/step-1.html

PASS Program by Dr. Francis Ihejirika, founder and CEO of PASS Program http://passprogram.net

Doctors in Training
http://www.doctorsintraining.com/

Boards Boot Camp for COMLEX ?
http://www.Boardsbootcamp.com/level1.php

Question Banks

- USMLE World Question Bank (2,045 questions): www.usmleworld.com

- Kaplan Question Bank (2,400 questions): www.kaplanmedical.com

- USMLERxQmax (3,000 questions): www.usmlerx.com

- COMBANK- for COMLEX (1,000 questions): http://www.combankmed.com

Assessment Tests

- NBOME COMSAE (Comprehensive Osteopathic Medical Self-Assessment Examination: http://www.nbome.org/comsae.asp

- NBME Self-Assessment Exam: https://nsas.nbme.org/nsasweb/servlet/mesa_main

- KAPLAN Question Bank Self-Assessment (included in the question bank)

Online Resources

- **Future Teaching Physicians—online medical community:** http://www.ftpinc.org

- **WebPath: The Internet Pathology Laboratory Free (online version):** http://library.med.utah.edu/webpath/

- **Pathology website: John Barone, MD:** http://www.baronerocks.com

- **Surgisphere Cooperation Clinical Review,** USMLE Step 1 Review, USMLE 3- digit score calculator: http://www.clinicalreview.com/solutions/resources/usmle-score-calculator.html

- **USMLE SCORE Correlation, USMLEWorld-Kaplan Qbank-NBME Score correlation** by Applicant Guide Team-http://usmle-score-correlation.blogspot.com

Comprehensive Review Books

- *First Aid Cases for the USMLE Step 1* Tao LE ISBN 9780071601351

- *USMLE Step 1 Secrets* BROWN ISBN 9780323054395

- *MedEssentials for the USMLE Step 1* MANLEY Kaplan Publishing; 3rd edition (December 1, 2009), 2010 ISBN 1607144824

By Subject

Anatomy and Embryology

- *High-Yield Neuroanatomy,* FIX Lippincott Williams and Wilkins, ISBN 9780781779463

- *High-Yield Embryology,* DUDEK ISBN 9780781768726

- *USMLE Road Map: Gross Anatomy,* WHITE ISBN 9780071445160

Behavioral science

- *High-Yield Behavioral Science,* FADEM ISBN 9780781782586

- *High-Yield Biostatistics,* GLASER ISBN 9780781796446

- *Underground Clinical Vignettes: Behavioral Science,* SWANSON Lippincott Williams and Wilkins, 2007, ISBN 9780781764643

Biochemistry

- *Lippincott's Illustrated Reviews: Biochemistry,* CHAMPE Lippincott Williams and Wilkins. 2007, ISBN 9780781769600

Microbiology

- *Clinical Microbiology Made Ridiculously Simple,* GLADWIN Med Master. 2007, ISBN 9780940780811

- *Microcards Flash Cards,* HARPAVAT Lippincott Williams and Wilkins. 2007. ISBN 9780781769242

Pathology

- *Rapid Review: Pathology,* GOLJAN Mosby 3rd edition ISBN 0323068626

- *BRS Pathology*, SCHNEIDER Lippincott Williams and Wilkins, 2009, ISBN 978078177941

Pharmacology

- *Lange Pharmacology Flash Cards,* BARON McGraw-Hill, 2009, 189 flash cards, ISBN 9780071622417

- *Lippincott's Illustrated Reviews: Pharmacology,* HARVEY Lippincott Williams and Wilkins, 2009. 564 pages, ISBN 9780781771559

Physiology

- *BRS Physiology,* COSTANZO Lippincott Williams and Wilkins, Lippincott Williams and Wilkins; Fifth, North American Edition (July 30, 2010) ISBN-10: 0781798760

Osteopathic Manipulative Medicine

- *OMT Review 3rd Edition,* Robert G. Savarese, ISBN 0967009014

References

LeTao, BhushanVikas, and Grimm Lars. *First Aid for the USMLE Step 1* 2009: *A Student to Student Guide,* McGraw-Hill Medical; 19th edition 2008

Adeleke T. Adesina

Adeleke earned his Bachelor of Science in biochemistry and general biology (summa cum laude) from Bloomfi eld College in 2008. He is currently a fourth-year medical student at the University of Medicine and Dentistry New Jersey, School of Osteopathic Medicine. He is the founder of Future Teaching Physicians Inc (FTPInc), an online community for medical professionals. His career interest is in emergency medicine. Adeleke scored 225/97 on his USMLE.

Farook W. Taha

Farook is a fourth year medical student at the University of Medicine and Dentistry New Jersey, School of Osteopathic Medicine. After graduating early from high school, he earned an associates degree in liberal arts and science at Dutchess Community College. Farook then transferred to Stony Brook University in New York and completed his bachelor's degree (summa cum laude) in chemistry. He is the co-founder of Future Teaching Physicians Inc (FTPInc), an online community for medical professionals. Farook scored 248/99 on his USMLE.

Adeleke and Farook are fulfilling the dreams of studying medicine and becoming physicians. They hope that others will be inspired by the tips they share in this publications.